Timeless Luminosity

Robert Aho

TIMELESS LUMINOSITY

The photo on the front cover was taken by Robert Aho, at his home.
Copyright © 2020

The painting on the back cover was created by Robert Aho, as part of the impossible task of exploring the visual aspects of his Near Death Experience.
Copyright © 2019

Published by Robert Aho

Duluth, Minnesota, USA

ISBN: 9798633736199

DEDICATION

With undying gratitude, to my Dzogchen root gurus,

Chögyal Namkhai Norbu Rinpoche and Keith Dowman,

as well as my many other Buddhist teachers, and their lineages,

Lama Dudjom Dorjee (Kagyu),

His Holiness the Dalai Lama (Gelug),

Roshi Steve Hagen (Soto Zen),

Khenpo Sherab Sangpo (Nyingma),

Lama Padma Gyatso (Nyingma),

Her Eminence Mindrolling Jetsün Khandro Rinpoche (Nyingma),

as well as His Holiness Sakya Trizin (Sakya).

Without each of my teachers, I would not have been able to create such poems as this, nor describe such experiences of the inexplicable.

They each have my eternal gratitude.

May all beings benefit.

TIMELESS LUMINOSITY

TABLE of CONTENTS

Author's Note		i
Proem		ii
Becoming Light		1
Luminous Mala		13
Timeless Luminosity		27
Dharmakaya Guru		31
Sambhogakaya Guru		33
Nirmanakaya Guru		34
1	Dreams	35
2	HRIH Happiness	35
3	Listen!	37
4	Beings who Slumber	38
5	Ocean of Suffering	38
6	Luminosity	39
7	Refuge of Mind	40
8	Sunrise Path	41
9	Radiant Path	41
10	Rain	42
11	Horizons Lost	43
12	Natural State	44
13	Kaya Song	44
14	What is Happening Here?	45
15	Inside	46
16	Luminosity	47

17	Consciousness	48
18	Clear Moment	49
19	Clarify this Moment	49
20	Examine this Life	50
21	Grasping at Illusion	51
22	Distractions	52
23	This Breath	53
24	Finding Peace	53
25	Discover Faith	54
26	Between Death and Death	55
27	We Have Ourselves	56
28	This Life	57
29	Look at mind.	59
30	Pure Intention	60
31	Jumbled Mess Monkey Mind	61
32	Many Who Seek	62
33	Rebirth	62
34	Death	64
35	Mind	66
36	Painful Heart	67
37	Dream Laughter	67
38	This Illusion Within	68
39	Relax, Just Relax	69
40	Dream Beginnings	70
41	This Impermanent Everything	71
42	Virtue Wisdom	72

43	Empty Cognizance	73
44	Reflecting Our Nature	75
45	Each Action	76
46	Discovering Freedom	77
47	Karmic Illusions	79
48	Beguiled by Causes	80
49	Eternal Moment	82
50	Holding onto Life	83
51	See the Ultimate	86
52	Take Refuge in the Ultimate	87
53	The Key to Everything	89
54	Enlightenment Intention	92
55	Awakening in this Moment	94
56	The Easiest Thing	94
57	Wandering Mind	97
58	Within a Very Long Dream	98
59	Examine Appearance	99
60	Death is an Illusion	100
61	Pure Vision	101
62	Being Patient	102
63	Seeking What Is	103
64	Clouds of Mind	104
65	Just This, Just That	105
66	True Intention	106
67	Pay Heed!	108
68	Understanding Our Condition	109

69	Infinite Blessings	111
70	Practice the Ultimate	112
71	Becoming Ultimate Light	114
72	This Trinity	115
73	Ultimate Guru	116
74	Guru at Death	117
75	Gurus	118
76	Awareness	119
77	Goodness Continues	120
78	Omnipresent That	121
79	Amazing Light	122
80	Immutable Peace	123
81	Liberating Oblivion	124
82	Perfect Moment	125
83	Preparing for Death	126
84	Life Beyond Explanation	127
85	Placing the Label	128
86	Swirling Madness	129
87	Timeless Expanse	130
88	Unbound Luminosity	130
89	Like a Golden Pearl	131
90	This Arc of Light	132
91	Indescribableness	133
92	Becoming Beyond	134
93	Within Expansive Now	135
94	Extreme Explosive Brilliance	136

95	Funny Moment	137
96	Immutable Essence	138
97	Remaining Timelessly Luminous	139
98	Pristine State	140
99	Timeless Wisdom	141
100	Bliss Unending	142
101	Unlimited Potentiality	143
102	Illuminated All	144
103	Sleeping Buddhas	145
104	Dharmakaya	146
105	Sambhogakaya	147
106	Nirmanakaya	149
107	Utter Luminous Joy	150
108	Timeless Bright Sky	152
Afterwards		155
Song of the Vajra		158
Acknowledgments		159
Referenced, Related & Recommended		160
About the Author		161

AUTHOR'S NOTE

Much of this work contains secret and restricted ways of looking at things. If individuals find themselves becoming disturbed, it is up to them to find teachers who can help with that. It is important to take responsibility for one's own spiritual practice. I did not write this with any boundaries, constraints or limitations. It is part of a samaya, or promise, that I have made, spanning lifetimes. What appears is a genuine, fully open, spiritual expression of my own experiences, meant to be encountered with presence of mind, openness and relaxation. May all who read or hear find benefit.

PROEM

This work began shortly after my own Near Death Experience in 2016. I remained quiet about what had happened for a while, thinking that it might be damaging for people to know what awaits them when they die, or if they got the wrong idea about it, that it might drive them mad or turn them into suicidal nihilists. The truth remains, despite my very best efforts, that death cannot be adequately described. It is truly beyond our feeble human minds to understand, unless we awaken.

It also occurred to me, as I began churning out poetry, rewriting prose on the subject, that this idea of describing what has just happened, when we have a Near Death Experience, is, perhaps, both ludicrous and complete folly. Many times, I stopped and really questioned just what it is that I am doing, why I am writing about death. What many people will tell you, if you were to ask them about their NDE, is that it can't really be described, it goes beyond description, it happens without concept, it was utter and complete knowing, much more real than reality. The light was so magnificent that nothing can compare, there is nothing whatsoever that comes close. It is like trying to describe reality to the insane. Why bother?

My first essay rendition of this attempted to address people from various faiths and scientific outlooks, trying to merge the vocabulary and express it in comparative terminology and concepts. This proved to be more than muddled. The vocabulary simply was not there that I needed. Neither science, nor mainstream Western cultures, nor most major religions really, had an adequate way of dealing with it, with death. Christianity comes close, only if love and compassion are not cluttered with other beliefs, and if we consider ourselves to be inseparable from the wisdom light of God. Science also comes close, only if we consider ourselves to be a quantum event, just energy consciously expressing itself; however, that loses what is most pertinent. Although the quantum experience is quite relevant, the most important element is love and compassion, which springs from the light. The quantum falls short of that at this time.

At some point, after several revisions, expanding and expounding, I decided that my only way forward would be to deal with this subject utilizing Buddhist terminology, which was quite readily available; and, more specifically, it became apparent to me that I needed to also utilize some terminology unique to Dzogchen in order to describe certain elements of the inexplicable. There was no reason to try to invent something new, the vocabulary was already there, well-established and readily available to people in all parts of the world.

Since the vocabulary of Dzogchen deals directly with experience that is beyond concept, it became clear that this was the best way I could move forward with the work I had in mind. It also became clear that the medium needed to have both a focused logic to it, as well as something more impressionistic, so that it could be available to everyone, without becoming too bogged down, requiring more in-depth study. The work needed to be something that helps the reader to settle into something most profound, that may not have been previously considered.

The following is both prose and poetry. It is meant to be taken in as a complete work in a general way, in order to form more of a big picture, for general understanding. Specific elements should not be reified in any way. If it is taken literally or as material object, then it will be misunderstood completely. It is best to just relax when reading the work, allow your natural intuitive abilities to be your guide. It is not meant to be an intellectual discovery, requiring years of study. It is meant to be a discovery of the heart, seeing that we have all been there. We've been here all along. Death is not unusual, we are all quite familiar with that.

The idea of a mala is also inherent in the structure of the poetry collection. Each poem is meant to be complete in and of itself; however, the poems should be read together in just the same way that meditation occurs while using mala beads. Each poem is set in a logical order, which can also bring benefit reading in reverse order. Contemplation occurs over and over again, reading and rereading is necessary. The first four poems form the guru beads of a mala. These are the four kayas: Svabhavikakaya, Dharmakaya, Sambhogakaya, and Nirmanakaya. All other poems, 108 in all, form meditations derived from these four gurus, who are one.

My life is very ordinary, nothing to see here, no reason to keep reading, if that is what you are looking for. My experiences are not particularly unusual. The work is derived from a perspective that has many influences. I am not a lama, nor do I want to be one, as title has little bearing on spiritual insight. I don't fancy myself as some hippie-cool practitioner of the Dharma that everybody should listen to, nor would I want that sort of fake ego-gratification. I do not live on top of a mountain, though I am reclusive. There is nothing extraordinary about me, or my life; and, there is nothing here in this text that should fascinate you in any way. I'm just ordinary.

All that is enclosed is not really something that you do not already know.

"We are what we think. Everything we are arises from our thoughts. With our thinking we create the world."

~Shakyamuni Buddha~

"All beings have lived and died and been reborn countless times. Over and over again they have experienced the indescribable Clear Light. But because they are obscured by the darkness of ignorance, they wander endlessly in a limitless samsara."

~Padmasambhava~

"Realization is not knowledge about the universe, but the living experience of the nature of the universe. Until we have such living experience, we remain dependent on examples, and subject to their limits."

~ Chögyal Namkhai Norbu Rinpoche ~

"Obsessive use of meditative disciplines or perennial study of scripture and philosophy will never bring forth this wonderful realization, this truth which is natural to awareness, because the mind that desperately desires to reach another realm or level of experience inadvertently ignores the basic light that constitutes all experience."

~ Tilopa~

"Without thinking that death will come, I am absorbed in plans for the future. After having done the many and futile activities of this life I will leave utterly empty-handed. What a blunder; as I will certainly need an understanding of the excellent dharma. So why not practice now?"

~Padmasambhava

"Oh son, watch the illusory spectacle!
All birth and death is projected by delusion, not existing in reality.
I am beyond coming and going."

~ Dzongsar Khyentse Chokyi Lodro~

"When one comes to the essence of being, the shining wisdom of reality illumines all like the cloudless sky."

~Milarepa~

"If, upon looking outwards towards the external expanse of the sky, there are no projections emanated by the mind, and if, on looking inwards at one's own mind, there is no projectionist who projects [thoughts] by thinking them, then, one's own mind, completely free from conceptual projections, will become luminously clear."

~Padmasambhava~

"If you want to know your past life, look at your present condition.
If you want to know your future life, look at your present actions."

~ Padmasambhava ~

"We're all going to die, all of us, what circus! That alone should make us love each other but it doesn't. We are terrorized and flattened by trivialities, we are eaten up by nothing."

~Charles Bukowski~

BECOMING LIGHT

It is, perhaps, very simple, this experience of death. Though we think we are solid, we are really only conscious energy, empty of any sort of material substance, timeless, luminous, and we are always in transition. Everything, every part of us, is in motion, our bodies, our thoughts, this notion of self, every atom, our environment—all of it, except that we are not limited to our bodies nor our notions of self. Even to say we are energy is not completely true. We are beyond that, inexplicable, ineffable, radiant. We are beyond all things. Our real nature defies explanation.

It is as if we are composed of billions of little swirling eddies of bright light, tiny whirlpools of rainbows and song, casting beams of light into the cosmos, vibrations within a spacious field of timeless brilliance. Each and every aspect of what we think we are does not stay the same from one moment to the next. We become something entirely new in the next moment, though we are not that either, as we are not the particles or the thoughts that appear in this swirling magical display. We can't be located. We, not being anything in particular that we can point to, are in a state of constant flux and change; and, yet, we seem to think we are solid and sort of permanent, more or less.

This is what keeps us from our own awareness about our real condition, this ignorance of what is timelessly luminous. We forget this knowledge that we are in a constant state of transition and change, knowing that we are living an illusion, grasping at any beliefs that can offer temporary comfort. By being ignorant about just what is going on here, we miss it. We transmigrate with each moment; yet, we think we are somehow a material being, limited to our soon-to-be waning body. This ignorance about our true condition keeps us from seeing our own potentiality. It keeps us fixated on what is not real, nor substantial in any way.

The whole universe is the same way, changing, transitioning, spinning, vibrating, always moving, recombining, never the same from one instant to another, filled with sentient beings who are mesmerized by all the confusion of this magical display. It happens everywhere, nowhere, both, neither, in this all-at-once-forever display of change, and we are largely oblivious to that. Though it is as obvious as can be, we don't see it. We miss the nature of our very existence, that great big magical eternal brilliance beyond thought. We miss it.

Amazing.

Not too long ago, I died. This is nothing extraordinary. Everybody dies. Usually, people don't remember dying. Usually, people don't remember being born or the dreams they have, either. It's difficult to remember this life, or past lives, or future lives, or what happened between one life and the next, or even what we had for breakfast. This is perfectly normal.

As part of a heart procedure, my heart stopped, I flatlined for a few minutes, and I turned to light during that experience, for an eternity. I was in that state for an eternity. I didn't go into the light, I became light. The light and I were completely the same, not different in the least, completely at rest and okay with that. I was completely integrated into the most amazing, brilliant, bright light imaginable. Actually, it was far beyond imagination. And to think of it as merely being light, as perceived by human eyes, is to fall far short of the actual experience. This light was far more intense than anything we can reasonably imagine. It was timeless, it was beyond all spatial constraints, beyond the universe, it was being consciously aware and ultimately compassionate, it was beyond any thought, object or concept. There was no me at this point.

Then, I returned to this person I had been, almost forgetting that I had been a person. It was very simple. The whole experience was very ordinary; however, I vividly remembered what had happened, and my life has become opened to that in every way.

It is often the case that a Near Death Experience creates a real crisis for the individual, as demonstrated in testimony after testimony. What was once thought of as a concrete, materially permanent reality, our life on earth, becomes something entirely different. Like a dream, what we had thought was reality has now come into question, becoming severely in dispute, falling apart entirely, appearing as something entirely unexpected. We see our lives as part of this magical illusion, with nothing solid about it. In many cases, because of this realization, a very serious crisis of beliefs emerges. We grasp at anything, search for meaning—and we come up short. We have discovered that belief is completely useless.

In general terms, people often describe a sense of bliss, of eternal love and compassion. This experience can be so joyful that people cry when they think about it. It leaves them speechless, because it is so much more than anything we are prepared to encounter. The experience is more real than what we think reality is, it is completely indescribable. It is the experience of omniscient awareness, of eternity, of all that is and all that is beyond. Death brings us to who we really are, timeless luminosity, which is home.

Many people miss the experience of death so much that they spend a very long time feeling very sad that they had to return to this life. It is not easy to understand the meaning of life after having all of our previous notions utterly destroyed, or that there could even be a point to any of it. We are left wondering what our fragile miniscule life really can mean in the context of being human, seeing the futility of our beliefs, this fictitious notion of self and our feeble human grasping at any sort of explanation. People returning to their ordinary lives lament that they cannot truly describe the experience, though it remains very strong in their mind. This is very typical. I myself went through a short period like this, feeling completely disoriented, and quite sad.

Everything we had previously believed enters a crisis. How could it not? Whereas we were previously moving innocently throughout our lives, ignorantly guarding our identity, creating beliefs about this and about that, protecting ourselves, our body and those close to us, defending everything that we thought was us, when, suddenly, we realize that this is not so important. We learn that it is just an illusion, a figment of our own imagination, a fabrication of mind that we, ourselves, have created. We realize that we are merely imagining ourselves and our life. It is all a figment of our own imagination; however, it is not nothing.

We also learn that everything springs from great compassion and love, as an amazing magnificent light. We learn that everything will be fine, it is all good. It is perfect. This idea of self that we had worked so hard to invent, becomes something that seems so ridiculously naive, something that is not really something; and, yet, it is connected, not separate, from everything else. We encounter primordial wisdom, and our idea of self utterly dissolves into that. This is one experience that is guaranteed to shake your notion of reality. Everything will be shaken to its core.

This was not so much the case with my own Near Death Experience, as I was only briefly disoriented and felt lethargic for a short time. Being completely shaken by the experience was transitory, very brief. In my case, laughter brought me back to a more stable condition, where I did understand that life is like a dream; and, yet, I remained quite relaxed within this knowledge.

Having always been a very serious seeker of spiritual wisdom, intense by all accounts, I had prepared myself to receive this gift of death and returning. Even with this preparation, I was truly shaken to the core. When I became integrated with timeless luminosity, there was no me, at least nothing that I had fabricated as me. This does tend to have a little impact on a person, when you realize you're not really there, and there's not really a there there.

In 2016, as I mentioned, I underwent a heart procedure, and a Near Death Experience joyfully appeared in my life. I have been very reluctant to talk about it for the most part, understanding how what I say could be easily misunderstood, which could lead to problems for the individual on their spiritual path. And I must say that every spiritual path is so very important; therefore, I would not want to imply that one path is better than another, or to discourage anyone from pursuing what has already brought them benefit. It was, however, eventually pointed out to me that it really is not up to me, that this is a gift that I must bring to others, if I can, if I have the ability to do so.

I had not previously considered this. The experience did not belong solely to me. It really belonged to everyone and beyond everything, because it is a common experience. So, the question is, how can I explain what happened without causing harm? How can I explain what is really unexplainable? This is quite a dilemma.

When I realized very clearly that I was not separate from anything else, nor was I something other than that intense timeless luminosity, I realized that this experience is something we all have had, whether we have had an NDE or not, whether we can remember or not. It happens between our lives, and at times of trauma. It happens when we have an epiphany and in dreams. It is not uncommon, I realized, it is ordinary.

As a background to the idea of having prepared myself for death, I was raised Lutheran, insisting that my Mother read the bible to me when I was just a toddler. Then, while still a child, I became very interested in other brands of Christianity, finding myself fascinated by the texts that were held as sacred, reading everything I could, including the complete Christian Bible, by my early teens. In time, after a little rebellion on my part, I became firmly Agnostic, not willing to accept the opinion of anyone else without proof. This was by my mid-to-late-teens, when I began focusing very strongly on Western science, and also exploring many religions and philosophies, as well as a brief encounter with Shamanism.

Eventually, I committed myself to Buddhism, which occurred when I realized that Buddhism was not really about belief, it was about knowing, it was about exploring direct experiences of mind. This makes sense, in my case, because I did not want to reject religion and I did not want to reject science, understanding that my spiritual path could neither limit nor reject such explorations of the mind. Both, it seemed to me, are looking at the same thing, just in a different way. His Holiness the Dalai Lama has said that a spiritual path must include the quantum, and he has done tremendous work integrating the questions of science with the direct spiritual observations of Buddhism. That same approach became the key for me. I was completely dedicated and devoted to Buddhism after realizing that. Eventually, I became a practitioner of Dzogchen, which is considered to be Buddhist or Bon, and is about direct experience with the ineffable nature of the mind, becoming aware throughout the day and night of our real nature. This is probably why I could remember the entire experience so clearly. I had prepared myself for that.

All of these spiritual explorations were very essential and important to me; so, I would likewise encourage others to become seekers of wisdom on a spiritual path that is specific to your needs, keeping an open heart and mind, without clinging to belief or limiting yourself in any way. Examine everything closely. Realize that truth can never be damaged by a question.

Having said that, I would also encourage you not to reject what you discover on your spiritual path, rather to lovingly embrace it as a part of what you learn, in order to mature in your own spiritual practice. The destination is not nearly as important as the Path. When something no longer fits your purpose, then let it go, it will no longer be of value; yet, lightly hold on to it for the time that it is good for you and as long as you find some benefit.

If someone were to ask me what to do, I would not tell them to follow what I have done, I would say that they should do what makes sense to them, and to commit themself to some sort of spiritual practice that has as its basis great compassion and love. If it does not have love and compassion as its main component, then it is of absolutely no value. It doesn't have to be religion or have religion at its base, it has to be spiritual practice that involves your life, not an idea of you; rather, it must be honestly connected to your circumstances, the life you are living, where you are, how your consciousness works, as well as how you perceive the world around you. If it is time to move on, do so with love and compassion for yourself and others. At some point, it does become obvious that the source of love and compassion is universal.

As a Buddhist, I have received knowledge and training about death and the nature of mind through numerous Buddhist teachings, from many teachers who were from many traditions, through dreams, and as part of a scholarly pursuit. My main practice, at the time of my Near Death Experience, as I indicated, was Dzogchen, though I also visited practices from various

Buddhist traditions based in Sutra and Tantra, from time to time. Simple meditation, focusing on breath, is still of great and precious value to me. Meditating on death and impermanence is ongoing, and I find it to be supremely important.

The practices of Hinayana, Mahayana, and Vajrayana never leave me, despite mainly practicing as a Dzogchenpa. I'm not a teacher, I'm more like a bit of a hidden yogi. I no longer seek teachings, having received what I need, there is no point, other than from time to time it is nice to go see people, to see how they are doing. I have just what I need, just as I am, living in a remote place in a northern forest. When practicing anything, and at all times as well, my life is really the practice of Dzogchen, and Dzogchen is something that cannot be constrained by notions of religion, spiritual practice or even concept. This is why I am explaining spiritual practice in this way. I see the value of not being constrained, but rather doing what is right for you, which can mean any number of possibilities. For many years I attended retreats, sought great teachers and received empowerments and transmissions from them. This was very important to me, and I am most fortunate that I was able to do that. And, I am very grateful to each and every one of them.

The complete Buddhist path has become so amazing to me, and I cannot say that one part of it is better than another. All levels of practice are equally important and amazing. The Hinayana is the foundation and the doorway to other teachings, so maybe that is the most amazing part of Buddhism, though I can only speculate. Perhaps it is the Mahayana, because that goes directly to the essence of ultimate truth by focusing on altruism, love and compassion. Perhaps the Vajrayana is best, because it transforms this illusion of the world of suffering. Imagine being a person encountering the Buddha, someone who had faced death by nearly starving, exposed to ultimate truth like that twenty-six hundred years ago.

Buddha Shakyamuni did something so amazing when he began with the Hinayana teachings, giving people a strong foundation like that, giving them a vehicle for becoming liberated. It made it possible for people to awaken, when starting that way, by simply understanding that we suffer and that there is a path away from that, by teaching people to practice by starting with your own issues, finding peace and happiness in a simple way, working with your own mind like that. Those first teachings of the Buddha were pretty amazing and very easy for anyone to understand. All Buddhists practice the Hinayana, it is where they take refuge and if forms the basis of all of their practice. It seems to me that starting with a strong foundation is very important. The Theravada school, which is the last remaining school within the Hinayana, has done some amazing things and helps so many people. If you are new to Buddhism, and are interested in learning, I would suggest starting there.

It also seems obvious that a person should move on and evolve in their spiritual practice, if they have the capacity for that. It's not essential. A person can receive tremendous benefit by simply practicing one thing for their entire lifetime. What is most important is to practice what is right for your spiritual path in this moment. Pray and meditate every day and night. Focus on love and compassion, and contemplate death. Sit in contemplation of life, and death. Let the light grow within you, open your heart and mind to the possibilities. Don't be egotistical about it, live and let live, be open and accepting of others. Find a good teacher. It is essential to find a good teacher to help guide you on your journey to where you are.

It is said by many teachers in Buddhism that the best spiritual practice is to practice where you are. One does not need to become a Buddhist to do that. One needs to be very honest to do that. It doesn't work if you are fooling yourself. We need to be honest, when it comes to spiritual practice, or there is no point.

One great advantage, in having been a Buddhist practitioner at the time of my death, is that it provided for a very precise vocabulary and intellectual context, tremendously useful tools, regarding passage through the stages of death, our states of mind, various experiences we might have and how we embody various qualities. This meant that I had the ability to go directly into that experience, remember what had happened and then describe it to others, for their benefit, if they were interested. Buddhism prepares us for the bardos in a way where we can remain relaxed and just experience the inevitable with joy and confidence, seeing it as it is, being very relaxed. That can be very good for our transmigration through the bardo of death, or this gap between lives.

My main spiritual teachers, nine in all, come from each of the major schools in Tibetan Buddhism and one from Soto Zen. The Dzogchen lineages are a little bit hard to understand; however, they are essentially Tibetan in origin in the Buddhist sense, having connections to Bon traditions, having strong influence from Garab Dorje, Padmasambhava and Vairocana, with roots going back to an unknown time prior to Buddhism, many thousands of years prior, or even further, maybe no beginning. I say these are my main teachers because I was able to receive spiritual practices from them and I implemented them into my daily life and dreams through meditation. Two of my teachers came to me as Dzogchen masters and gave me essential teachings on that. They became my root teachers, because of how they transmitted Dzogchen teachings to me.

Some of the teachings on death that I have received, such as Phowa and Zhitro, are considered restricted, usually requiring special permission from a qualified teacher, simply because the student must be ready to receive this knowledge. Other practices are more openly available. With this knowledge, I very diligently practiced meditation on death, both my own and in helping others when they pass, as well as impermanence and the preciousness of this human life. Some of the Dzogchen practices involve very deep contemplation, where the luminous state of mind is experienced directly.

During the day, I diligently spent at least some time meditating, even when I was busy, usually first thing in the morning and just before bedtime. Sometimes I would spend many hours per day meditating. At night, I practiced dream yoga, in my dreams, whenever possible. This is a practice that can be learned by first knowing how to lucid dream and then by applying practices of meditation to that. Because of this lucidity in my dreams, I learned amazing things just in the dream state alone. There is perhaps much more to say about dream yoga; however, it prepared me for the experience of death and I thought I should mention it briefly.

Every chance to be diligent and to persevere in my practice, every opportunity, both day and night, I would receive teachings, study, meditate, contemplate, keep this knowledge and bring myself back to a peaceful state when I became disturbed or distracted. My life didn't really appear to be odd. I lived my life in what seemed to be a normal life, appearing to be ordinary, participating in life, being silly, eating food, concentrating on work and my profession, experiencing pain, spending time with friends and family, while keeping my spiritual practice in mind at all times. For certain, and every day, I also spent a great deal of time sitting on a cushion meditating. This is how I prepared.

So, in order to bring benefit to even one person, I would like to share my experience in as honest and open a manner as possible:

My heart had some structural and electrical problems that were giving me problems and needed attention; so, I found myself at the hospital, undergoing a fairly routine procedure. As the procedure room filled with people and anesthesia was administered, I recall hearing a voice telling me that I should wave. This seemed very odd to me. I'm not entirely sure if this was actually someone in the room, maybe the anesthesiologist, or maybe just my imagination. It didn't matter to me; so, I waved goodbye.

In a moment or so, very suddenly, I became bright light for an eternity.

It was not me in light, I was bright clear light, extremely intense, inseparable from me, pervasive, infinite, beyond all concept and reason. Instantaneously, I became infinite wisdom and clarity, completely conscious, open, empty, luminous. In that moment, there really was no me, the idea was, in fact, quite preposterous. I have heard it said that this is vast luminosity of mind or the nature of mind. That explanation does not even begin to do it justice. People also love to explain this sort of experience with religion or science, which is utterly preposterous. This is raw experience of reality. Any concept at all does not come close, seeming to merely point in its direction, not even touching the surface of this direct experience, missing the reality altogether.

Directly experiencing reality is not something we are used to doing. Our habitual way of dealing with everything is to form beliefs, inventing our world around us, fixating on what is not real. This is why preparation for meeting the death experience was so important.

The light itself was so intense that nothing, not even the sun, can compare. The sense of bliss was beyond imagination; and, yet, all of this description does not do it justice. It was light beyond light, bliss beyond bliss, absolute everything beyond absolutely everything, timeless knowing beyond all knowing, eternity beyond time. It was the essence of our real nature, without any sort of human thought filtering or narrating. The idea of any idea, even no idea, lost all meaning. In essence, becoming the timeless luminous state was truly indescribable. It was the empty essence of ultimate truth, beyond all concepts. In Buddhist traditions, this is referred to as Dharmakaya, Luminous Dharmata or Buddha Nature, depending upon your point of view.

I remained in that state for a timeless eternity; though, time had no real meaning; so, I cannot really say whether it was an infinite array of time or an instant. It was conceptless time, beyond all measure. Linear time certainly vanished in any way that we know it. There was no me, I had no body or sense of self; though, it was not nothing that I became, because I became what is beyond everything. There was only this luminous state of awareness, omniscient presence of mind, which cannot be reified in any way. For that eternity of resting in the luminous state, I was home, where we all have been, where we all will be, where we have always been.

Slowly, slowly, sounds and colors joyfully began to appear in what seemed to be a very small place within that intense light of Dharmakaya. This is referred to as Sambhogakaya in Buddhist traditions, an energetic dimension. With the emergence of consciousness within the body of Sambhogakaya, I slowly remembered the idea about having ideas, this notion of concepts, this idea of self I had once understood, which now seemed so dull and far away. In this state, I was not thinking with concepts or language or words, or even ideas. Fixation on conceptual thinking had not yet emerged from this state. It was merely the essence of concepts which emerged in a delightful way, with little tiny swirls of vibration and colors, and light and rays, and joyful sound, which all turned out to be so much larger than our entire universe.

Then, suddenly, while contemplating the essence of all, the thought occurred that I must be seeing the universe here someplace. I remembered the universe when looking at all those colors, in a very dark corner of this magnificent array, when I began to fixate again in the normal way that beings fixate. My habitual mind came back to me very slowly in this way.

Immediately upon this thought, I noticed a much smaller place, very dark and dull, nearly microscopic by comparison to the Sambhogakaya dimension, which was, apparently, actually our universe, which seemed like a trace of a distant memory about a life where I had once manifested in a much smaller place still, almost microscopically imperceptible, the planet earth, and becoming aware of a body that had lived in a very small remote part of that very small obscure world.

I became cognizant of the empty luminous characteristics of Dharmakaya, and I also began to remember who I once had been, living a life on Earth. I could see that this manifestation, the combining of empty essence and cognizant nature, of Dharmakaya and Sambhogakaya, would bring about a familiar physical reality once again, the Nirmanakaya dimension, which is like a dream, magical in every way, illusory in all its aspects.

At first, once I began to consciously remember my life again, I thought that I didn't really want to go back to being that. It seemed like too much bother and even very painful, which instantly amused me. It seemed simple enough, I could just look away, not become fixated on that. With this thought, the sounds of laughter and rushing winds swirled about, and I realized that I must definitely bring myself back, as painful as it would be; so, I began with a practice called Ati Guru Yoga, by generating a specific symbol in my mind, then I chanted mantras, I formed mudras with my hands, I sang a song called the *Song of the Vajra*. These are practices mainly related to my root teacher, Chögyal Namkhai Norbu Rinpoche, who has since passed away. He directly transmitted this knowledge to me, and it is something I hold as quite precious.

I kept doing these practices very diligently for a very long time, without losing my focus, realizing that I was making a concerted effort to manifest once again, within an illusion that had once seemed so very real, my human life. I could sense this manifestation forming, this person I had once been. I could sense that this magical illusion was becoming almost as if it were real. This amused me so very much. Of course, it was not real! This whole life of daily living and dreams was obviously just an illusion.

After a very long time, I became aware of sounds in the hospital, and I could sense that I was breathing and that my body was warm. This luminous energy was still very strong, as it manifested within clear awareness, swirling around me, sparks of white light here and there. I remained diligent with my mantras and mudras, and song.

In the distance, I heard the nurses talking about me. I could hear that people were worried, then starting to become relieved by me coming back to them. Just then, I could feel that my hands were moving in motions which formed various mudras, and I could hear my voice chanting weakly, quietly. Slowly, slowly, I felt my body become integrated with the presence of my mind.

I could hear that the nurses were speculating about what they were witnessing. One of them asked another, "what on earth is he doing?" Another nurse speculated that I must meditate, or that I must be a Buddhist. Very suddenly my eyes opened and I laughed and said, "you could be right." Then, with a big smile on my face, I immediately asked, "could we do that again?"

The nurses laughed somewhat hysterically, people outside the room started laughing, somebody slapped a desk, other people rushed in to see. My heart doctor stood there with sweat dripping down from his face. Shaking his head very nervously, he said that he doesn't think we should ever do that procedure with me again. Several people laughed, all shaking their heads in agreement. No, they didn't think I should do that again. It was as if everything everywhere was joyful, even my doctor's anxiety seemed quite joyful. In this laughter, I had found great confidence in my spiritual practice.

It was very good. Everything was good. I understood with confidence.

I hesitated to say anything at first, then mentioned to the nurses that I think I must have died. When I eventually asked how long I was dead, they told me that I wasn't actually declared dead, though my heart did stop for a while. They showed me the heart monitor printout, pointing at what was shown, describing their worries about me, then becoming relieved when my heart began to move again. It showed my heart flatlining for a while, then slowly one very weak beat happened, then flatlining again, then slowly, slowly moving again, then slowly, very slowly starting to beat regularly, though still very weakly, increasing slowly, slowly, then slowly back to a normal rhythm. It took a while before it was beating regularly.

This was very surprising to me. I discovered that, in the procedure room, I had been gone for just five minutes, or so. This entire eternity of my departure was not really noticed by anyone but me. This world was just an illusion and the people in it didn't really notice anything that had been so intense in my experience. They just remained, innocently going through what they needed to do, remaining fixated on the task at hand, as if it were all real. And, here I was, suddenly going forward with confidence, knowing that I had never left the Dharmakaya state. This timeless luminosity still surrounds everything everywhere at all times, beyond what seems real in this life, even though this life is just ordinary.

Here I was in the physical dimension again, after an eternity, here I was breathing, with my heart beating, just like that. I couldn't help but laugh. This was just so funny. For what possible purpose could I be here again? I didn't know, and I'm still not certain that I need to be here.

The light looked different to me, colors, sounds, everything seemed completely different, it was not the same. I would visit places that I knew well, and they did not match my memories in the least. I was amazed that the light was now so dull, not nearly as vibrant or bright, as I remembered it. The death experience had been so much more intense. The sky beyond the clouds, where the sun shines brightly, could not compare.

And, so, going back into this life, not really having gone anywhere, not really having anywhere to go, I quietly contemplated what that was all about, going back to my meditation cushion, going back to my job and to my family, living a life again, being very reluctant to talk about what had happened, what my experience had been, confidently practicing again and again to remain in that awareness of our real nature.

This is how it was for me.

LUMINOUS MALA

Discussing my Near Death Experience, my telling of the details, happened only slowly. As I mentioned, I was worried about causing harm by revealing something that might be viewed as secret, something that might be misconstrued. It wasn't so much about what people might think about me, it was more that I might say something that might cause problems.

I wrote down the experience in both prose and poetry, finding the most satisfaction in poetry. At some point, I did share an essay with some people, though I was not very happy with it. It was difficult for me to simply open up about it, and I was finding it impossible to communicate, even if I made every concerted effort.

Although prose can really describe anything, sometimes we need to look for other ways to express what cannot be communicated with a logical description, or a straight-forward flurry of words, where people become lost and overwhelmed in all the elaborate subtlety. Poetry offers an avenue for expressing the inexplicable. This is why I have utilized not only prose, but also poetry as an expression of my Near Death Experience.

Poetry was really the first thing I created, after having my NDE. I began writing one poem after another, mainly keeping them secret, not wanting to talk to anyone about what had happened. Over and over again, then rewriting, then editing, sometimes throwing them away, the poetry kept evolving. It was important to me. It was part of my own discovery into what had happened.

With direct experience of the luminous condition, we narrate to ourselves about just what we have encountered. If it doesn't make sense to us, or if we find our beliefs in crisis, we create a narrative. This doesn't mean the narrative is correct, it means it gives us something to hang onto. With death, there comes a point when we can't narrate to ourselves, nor would we want to. We enter into an inexpressible state that just is. We can't really point to an object or any frame of reference, such as time or material reality. All of those human constructs simply disappear into the ineffable that is beyond human understanding.

The inexpressible elements of an NDE go beyond what can be described. The way we narrate about the experience limits our ability to really get to the core of that experience. Years before having my own Near Death Experience, I thought about creating a series of poems that could be used for meditative purposes, similar to how a mala is used, in order to really find a way through poetry into the depths of contemplation, that go beyond our own narration of the inexplicable. A mala is a string of beads, usually 108 beads, with a guru bead, which might consist of one or more beads together that appear in the same place together. Mantras are chanted in the circle of beads, going from the guru bead to the guru bead, but never over the guru. One merely reverses course, chanting over and over again, 108 times, reversing course every time the guru is met, potentially accumulating millions of mantras, through diligent effort in that way.

As I developed some health issues, some years ago, the poetry mala project encountered some major obstacles. Later, after my NDE, when I looked over all my work, I realized that this project must continue. That is when I changed the focus, calling it the *Luminous Mala*, which later became a part of this *Timeless Luminosity* project. This collection of poems focused on that bright experience of death, timeless luminosity, and all that this entails in our life, as well as awakening to our true potential.

Many of the older poems I had written were discarded, some were repurposed, as I realized they had some merit and significance to this project. To look at the following poems properly, one must see that they are really intended to be a complete work, not merely a collection of poems. The vocabulary, although written primarily in American English, delves occasionally into established Buddhist terms or expressions, which may have their basis in Sanskrit or Tibetan. I found it very necessary to utilize these terms, as the corresponding English terms were vastly inadequate, or required elaborate descriptions. The reality of describing and receiving such communication about an NDE necessitates that we truly understand ideas that verge on the limits of conceptual understanding, with a sort of relative ease. Buddhist terminology provides that very well, in this case.

The term *Buddha*, for instance, has no English equivalent. The term really means that it is one who dwells in a condition that is beyond conceptual constraints, one who has gone beyond, being completely aware of this moment, as well as the essence of all and the illusion that is our lives. This means that a Buddha is aware of that bright light we experience in death, as a continuous condition of our being, not just out there, but in every moment of life. The Sanskrit term for this timeless luminosity is *Dharmakaya*, which is also known as the mind of a buddha, which is the dimension of ultimate reality embodying truth. Dharmakaya, being one of the dimensions or aspects of a buddha, then became one of the guru poems in the string of poems. It is interesting to note that we all encounter this state of mind when we die. It is inevitable, even if we don't recognize what that is. It is our real primordial nature. Since we all encounter this, we all have a *Buddha Nature,* or have the potential in us to awaken and become aware of that amazing bright light of Dharmakaya in every moment, without having to go anywhere.

Now, with my own NDE, I became integrated into that Dharmakaya light for an eternity. This statement sounds a bit ludicrous, as it was only five minutes, or so, in the hospital where my body was located, where they saw me flatline. To me, from my relative point of view, however, I was gone for a timeless eternity. Also, from the ultimate point of view, I was timeless luminosity. Nothing indicated time, or any concept of anything at all, for that matter. The light itself, that insanely intense bright light, was more real than anything we think or call reality.

At that moment of eternity, I knew ultimate reality, the essence of all and beyond, just as we all do when returning or becoming aware of the state of timeless luminosity. Slowly, slowly, upon returning to my daily life, however, I realized that we have all been in this condition countless times. Then we are born into a body and we forget, becoming habituated by our own problems in life, getting old, dying, then returning to timeless luminosity, then becoming reborn once more. We're caught up in a whirlwind of our own mind, our own making.

We do this over and over again within cyclic existence, over countless eons, throughout infinite lifetimes, from beginningless beginnings. This existence really has no beginning and no end. It is a product of mind deluding itself from within this bright reality of Dharmakaya, which remains hidden to us. It is timeless, infinite in all directions, indescribable. The reality that we think is there existing, is just this illusion that we construct for ourselves.

I think that the only reason I had noticed this about the light, how we appear from the light, developing a cognizance along the way, was that the details remained with me, entirely vivid in my mind, sort of running in the background along with my daily life and dreams, appearing in the foreground through my continuing practice of the mind. It was only possible in this way because I have been a very devoted practitioner of the *Dharma,* or teachings of the mind which help us to discover what we might think of as reality, utilizing various meditative techniques both in dreams and in daily life, seeking useful ways to become familiar with and recognize timeless luminosity in each moment.

When I appeared out of that eternity, that timeless luminosity, Dharmakaya, while still remaining in that light, I could not easily remember that I had been a person at first. I was in an energetic condition, surrounded by bright colors and swirling manifestations, sounds like the rushing of wind, but also song among that. When I remembered my previous life, thought about it with dread, then I began to chant mantras in this turbulent atmosphere, forming mudras without a physical body, consciously bringing myself back into that body I remembered off in the distance. This energetic cognizant condition is referred to as *Sambhogakaya* in Sanskrit. It is bliss, the condition of perfect enjoyment, which is perceived only by Aryas, Bodhisattvas and Buddhas.

An *Arya* is an exalted one who has achieved a certain level of realization, for instance realizing nirvana, without completely becoming a Buddha. *Bodhisattvas* are those with a certain level of realization where they work to help others achieve complete awakening, or Buddhahood, before they themselves achieve complete Buddhahood, or ultimate awakening beyond the constraints of our worldly existence. Bodhisattvas are keenly aware of *Bodhicitta*, which is great compassion and the intention of becoming fully awakened. This same Bodhicitta is ultimately manifest in the light of Dharmakaya. It is ultimate truth, timeless luminosity infinitely radiating.

One may wonder why I utilized the term *Dzogchen* in the first of the four guru poems, since Dzogchen is generally considered to be secret. In reality, Dzogchen is the total perfection of our true condition, that which is ultimate reality. While Dzogchen teachings may be considered to be secret, the general characteristics of Dzogchen are very much the same as that timeless luminosity that we all experience, and that is not secret. As I indicated, we experience this each and every time we die. Only the teachings for accessing this light in our daily life are secret, requiring much preparation, usually many years in Buddhism, in order to avoid many potential traps and pitfalls. One must become a very devoted practitioner, or the whole exercise will become an act of futility.

Dzogchen is about bringing that luminosity into every moment of your day and night; thus, it was both essential and necessary to utilize this term as the teachings of the guru who permeates all aspects of our life and death. Dzogchen teachings are really very sudden and direct. We need to prepare for that, and that is the only reason why they are secret.

With me, however, I have no sectarian constraints. My practice cannot be called this or that. I am not beholden to a teacher, nor am I limited in any way. My experience is mine, and I have chosen to share what I have encountered in such a way that it can open up to us gradually or suddenly, as the needs of the individual permit. I see timeless luminosity as a condition of our true being, one that eludes us through lifetime after lifetime. We all know that eternal wisdom, and we all try to remember through spiritual practice and other means. Since our real condition is not really secret, there is no reason to say it is so.

In Buddhism, Sutra teachings were associated with our physical condition. The Buddha taught in an ordinary human form, speaking in a way that could be readily perceived by ordinary beings. In many ways, he, himself, was very ordinary. He was born into power and wealth, then realized it would not help him in the least. Then he chose a spiritual path, which also did not help, even though he had become one of the great practitioners. Before he became known as the Buddha, he found a way to go beyond, becoming aware of our pervasive condition of Dharmakaya.

Later, when people were ready to learn about transformation, Tantra became a teaching of more of an energetic understanding, only becoming available when people could understand. Although having existed previously in early Bon, some 14,000 years prior, Dzogchen was adopted by Buddhism, as the highest teaching, the Great Perfection. This teaching explored our real condition, timeless luminosity; and, although the teaching had been there during Buddha's teaching, it was very secret and not generally available. Only a small number of practitioners could receive benefit from such teachings, so people were not yet ready to learn about our timelessly luminous state, Dharmakaya, that they already knew only so well, but had forgotten, due to disturbing emotions and continuous distractions, as well as fixations on what is not real.

While Dzogchen might be equated with Dharmakaya, it is really associated with all of our ultimate condition, or Svabhavikakaya, which unites the three kayas. It is meant not only for our deeper explorations of mind; but, also, it is for everyday living, becoming aware of our real condition in a very pragmatic way, through each moment of our lives. It is meant to explore this notion of awakening for what is, as it is.

The first of my 'guru poems', *Timeless Luminosity*, required this vocabulary in order to provide some understanding of just what that is, providing an infinite setting amid beginningless beginnings. The poem is not about a guru in the traditional sense; rather, it is the timeless guru of our real condition. While we come from this timeless luminosity, we are also energetic and cognizant, as illustrated by the *Sambhogakaya*. We are also in a physical body, as per the *Nirmanakaya* dimension. So, the first guru unites all gurus of mind, speech and body, as well as Dharmakaya, Sambhogakaya and Nirmanakaya.

Mind is that illuminated emanation, which cannot be located, that we usually forget about when we go through our daily life and dreams. Speech is that energetic emanation that goes beyond our physical condition. Body is that physical emanation that we are all so very familiar with, our own world that we live in and this person, this self whom we mistakenly think is real.

Dzogchen, while entering awareness of the light of Dharmakaya through specific practices of the mind, perfecting how we gain access, self-liberating in this moment, also permeates our physical state, as well as our energetic condition, throughout every moment. This is the true meaning of Dzogchen, the Great Perfection. Dharmakaya, as it is understood, is really never separate from any aspect of our awareness, our lives, our actions, our being. This, I discovered, was key to remembering that incredibly brilliant timeless light beyond all, our real nature.

Although we are all quite familiar with that awareness, timeless luminosity, it is so very apparent that we quickly become caught up in the problems of our daily life, forgetting, through fixation, grasping and disturbing emotions, that we are beings of light, not really existing, not really not existing, between the extremes of existence and non-existence. This primordial wisdom is not something we can know intellectually, nor can it be discovered materially. It is beyond that, not requiring any special abilities to be in that knowledge. All we need do is relax, just be in our natural state, as it is.

Simple daily practices, as well as learning to relax and become aware within dreams, made it possible for me to remember the particular details of my particular NDE, which, as I stated previously, was actually fairly ordinary, not particularly unusual in any way. If you were to read many testimonials, you would discover aspects here and there that can also be found in my description. It is really quite amazing how very similar my description really is to what others have to say. I also discovered that the Tibetan Book of the Dead had close similarities, though I am, perhaps using slightly different methods to communicate.

I am simply describing what happened in a personal way that explores the details through poetry and prose, in a way that may be just a little bit unique, in that you can join that experience through reading and hearing the poems, while contemplating our condition. My explanation also does not delve into culturally specific elements, which are broadly understood in Tibetan Buddhism, but may have less relevance in the West. I didn't feel that there was a need to go into that very far, preferring simple language to that.

Each of the individual poems is a step for understanding timeless luminosity. My understanding of this is that we need to awaken, at least just a little bit, in order to see that knowledge, to become integrated with that. To become fully integrated with that light might require years of practice and meditative techniques, in order to be able to live with that knowledge in each moment; although, there is really no hard-fast rule that applies to everyone.

To integrate timeless luminosity, we can discover either sudden or gradual ways of approaching this knowledge. It can't be learned intellectually, it must be learned experientially. It does not really require intellect at all, it requires an open heart and mind, and a certain experiential capacity to receive such an amazing teaching of ultimate reality. People often become disturbed by the term capacity in Buddhism, thinking it means intelligence. It really means having an open heart and mind. The more open, the greater the capacity. We have the ability to increase our capacity. When we are fully open, when our capacity has no bounds, we awaken.

As I said previously, this timeless wisdom is encountered repeatedly throughout the infinite eons, in our beginningless cycle of life, death and rebirth. We see that bright light at times of trauma and at times of ecstasy. We see flashes of light in our dreams, when we are very open to that, while in that state of mind. We discover this timeless luminosity many times, even if we are startled.

We also don't usually remember such experiences for long, because we become obsessed with our lives, with our problems and grasping at explanations, as well as reifying that which is not real. To awaken to this ultimate knowledge is not some deep dark mystical achievement, it is just having a knowledge of this present moment and our real nature, without being distracted. This takes a little practice. Living in a way that is filled with light, not thinking that timeless luminosity is out there, out of your reach until you die or go beyond, or until you achieve something great, is really at the heart of awakening. It is very simple, very subtle, which is what makes it so very difficult. With habitual existence, we work very hard to create and defend what we think is real. Awakening is being open to a reality that requires no defense. It is as it is.

In Tibetan Buddhism, some of the great mystical practices involve learning how to awaken while passing through the death bardo. A *bardo* is just a gap in our cyclic existence; in this case, death is a gap between one lifetime and another where we encounter timeless luminosity in a very open way, among other elements of mind. It is said that we should train to recognize ıich is our primordial nature, discovering the primordial buddha ɔmantabhadra, who is not separate from us. If we can do that, we can remain in the light as fully awakened buddhas. While I agree with this, I would also add that there is absolutely no reason we can't awaken at any time, at any given moment, remaining in the light, even if we are burdened with a physical body. Putting this off into the future is completely unnecessary, if you are ready to open your heart and mind, if you have that sort of capacity. If you are ready, then it is time to open. If this is too much, then practice in order to become ready.

In some instances, the poetry of the *Luminous Mala* contains seed syllables. This was necessary, as the most direct expression made the most sense. *AH* is the symbol that represents our primordial nature, or timeless luminosity. In some sense, AH also relates to the energy we produce. *OM* represents the body or the universe. *HUM*, which is pronounced more like 'HOONG' represents mind. *HA* and *HO* both represent joyful laughter, both in our physical dimension and in an ultimate sense of joy. And, *HRIH* represents ultimate compassion.

In Tibetan Buddhism, seed syllables are often used in chanting mantras, but also in various teachings. These are generally considered secret; though, by that, what is really meant again is that people should prepare themselves to receive teachings about these, and receive transmissions or empowerments from a qualified teacher, or it could be easy to misunderstand what is meant. Behind all of these teachings is the intention that the teachings will be of benefit. I would encourage anyone to seek teachings from a qualified teacher, or many teachers, no matter what it is that you believe, even if you think your capacity is low. To learn even just a little bit will bring benefit for any number of lifetimes to come. Tibetan lamas typically teach in such a way that only enhances what you currently know. They do not, as a rule, proselytize, as that is generally harmful.

While each poem is meant to stand on its own, the string of 108 poems, together with the four guru poems, are meant to complement each other, potentially helping anyone who reads them, to open up their heart and mind to timeless luminosity. My thought in creating these poems was to provide one poem and then another that nudge this understanding just a little bit, helping to open up your capacity. When I was reading and editing them myself, I found that I benefitted by seeing new meanings that I had not consciously intended. This is another indicator of our intrinsic wisdom, our Buddha Nature.

Poetry has a way of leaving doors open, expanding horizons, bringing out meanings through emotionally vivid imagery. When I completed poem 108, I reversed order, edited and contemplated in the opposite direction. Poems which seemed difficult both to write and to read afterwards were much simpler the second time that I went over them. They became much clearer. I wanted more, I wanted to keep reading from front to back and from back to front, just like we do with a mala, when we are chanting with the use of a mala.

Perhaps these are merely a personal meditation, for my own benefit.

I truly hope that my simple work creates some benefit for at least one person. As I said, my Near Death Experience was nothing special, just an ordinary excursion into a bardo that we all know only too well. I would hope that my poetry might help to alleviate the yearning many people feel about returning to that ultimate condition, our home, that momentary awakening we experience when we die, through this knowledge.

Despite our yearning to return home, into timeless luminosity, we need to be patient and work with our circumstances. It has been said by many people, who have had an NDE, that it wouldn't work to simply commit suicide. We can't go back in that way. We would just come back again, and with the added burden of having committed suicide. That is some very heavy karma that is best to avoid. Committing violence against ourselves would not alleviate the frustration of living.

This frustration, as I have discovered, is not at all unusual, as life is very much filled with an uneasiness that just won't go away. People suffer so terribly in life. My thought in creating this work is that meditations on my poetry, contemplating our real condition, might be what we need. Maybe I am helping just a little bit. Through practice, it becomes possible to liberate our suffering into each moment. Liberating all suffering is my intention in creating this work, and in sharing my experiences of the death bardo.

I should also say a little bit, something extremely personal, about the form of these poems, as there is purposeful intention related to how they appear visually and with sound. It has been a bit difficult to reveal this to others, and I almost kept it buried, very secret, as it is also disturbing. The process of opening my heart and mind, however, leads me to share more than is typical, more than some say should ever be shared.

The fact that the poems are like a mala is important, as this reflects cyclic existence. These poems are contemplations about our real condition, not some superficial poetry meant to make us feel better. These poems will shake up your understanding, rearrange how you might think about death, rearrange your priorities in life. Death is very unsettling, as is glimpsing appearances as they truly are, realizing how truly disturbing this cycle of life and death and rebirth truly is. Nothing is stable or permanent.

Perpetual cyclic existence appears to us when we die, when we realize that we have gone and that now we are coming back. We see the world and we see how we are caught up in that. It's not a pleasant thing to witness. We may also catch glimpses of how we have been going through this cycle of birth and death and rebirth from beginningless beginnings and beyond. We might become aware of many lifetimes, as this is what happens when we become aware, even a little bit. Nothing remains hidden to us, as we think it might. We must face all of our demons, we must develop the courage to become indestructible. When we are timeless luminosity, for an eternity, while we are fully integrated with the light, there is nothing hidden. When we come back, we quickly clutter our lives again with all sorts of things, hiding what we need, creating more problems for ourselves without realizing it. Most things become hidden again.

Throughout my current life I could catch glimpses of how I died from my last lifetime, and I would meditate upon them throughout my life, starting at a very young age. When I was a child, I had a recurring dream, which I learned later was just the last few moments of my last life. It was about my death, before I realized I was dead. The dream was about fire and smoke, compression and release into space, being utterly compressed, then ultimately scattered to the winds. With my NDE, this became very clear. Each poem that I wrote after that experience took on this form, as sort of a contemplation into that last moment, and then the first moment of this life—songs of our real condition. Not only was the poetry about my Near Death Experience, it was also paying homage to that last lifetime, when I went unexpectedly through the death bardo, into this life.

In my last life, my parents were singing, just before I died. In my next life, this life, my parents were singing just after my birth. I discussed this with my father before he died, and he was amazed that I could remember. My mother confirmed that this had happened, that she and my father were singing when I was born, but doubted that it was something I had remembered, thinking that my father had told me. It is just too amazing to accept using our conventional way of seeing things, so another narrative filled that gap. The recurring dream, however, was about how I had previously died, which was from a bomb or artillery, in wartime, blown up by soldiers who were clearing the way. I remembered frantically trying to find my body amid the smoke and fire, which had suddenly taken me, scattered my body into disintegrated traces of what had been. The violence of that explosion was still ringing in my ears, as well, when I was reborn. It was really ringing in my mind when I was then born into my current person.

At the time of my death, from my last lifetime, I was just a small child in the Himalayas, helping to herd my family's animals away from Chinese soldiers, who were coming up through the valley where we lived. Prior to this, we, my family, had been expecting me to go meet a great teacher, maybe enter a monastery, but the invasion of our lands disrupted those plans. I recall my parents were so very proud of me, happy for the whole family, because it was very good to have a son in the monastery, sending me off to meet a great teacher. Even so, with soldiers invading our land, within eyesight, and with planes roaring overhead, my parents did not seem to think anything would happen to us, because of such amazing blessings that had been received and such good news, protections from the Buddha, it did not make sense that plans for my future could be stopped. It's possible that this may just have been how they were, so that I wouldn't become upset, I don't really know. My parents were singing songs of the Buddha, which were meant to help us feel safe, and then, BAM!, that was that, I was reborn on the other side of the world.

This raises the question, how can I know? The answer to that is that I cannot know anything, nor can anyone else know anything about anything, except for the timeless luminosity of Dharmakaya. And, even Dharmakaya cannot be known like some other measly human concept, it must be realized. That event of my past death simply left a very strong imprint upon me that I have been dealing with my entire life, working hard to avert anger, remembering glimpses, which strongly came to fruition following my NDE. I remembered not only my NDE, but also previous lifetimes and the way I had died just previously to this lifetime. It is why I wrote these poems, why I chose to write them in this way, and why I have decided to share them.

My true preference would be to simply fade away into obscurity. The world is a horrible place, filled with so much violence, so many ugly occurrences. I knew, however, that doing so is not really an option, it's not who I am. It is important for me to bring what I know to this place that is so embroiled in the poisons of mind, in order to help others find liberation, to help people awaken.

What really drove this project forward was the influence of Chögyal Namkhai Norbu Rinpoche, who had become one of my root teachers the year before my NDE. When I first met him, he gave me a copy of a poem, written in the Dakini language of Oddiyana, called the *Song of the Vajra.* No one really knows how old this song is. It is a song of liberation, containing all Dzogchen teachings, which is meant to be sung while in a state of deep contemplation. According to my teacher, it comes from the *Nyida Kajor,* which is the *Union of the Solar and Lunar Tantra.* It is also the main mantra found in the *Tibetan Book of the Dead,* also known as the *Bardo Thödrol.*

The Song of the Vajra is something I sing every single day, as it has very profound meaning to me. I have done so ever since learning the song, which was in the months following when I met Chögyal Namkhai Norbu Rinpoche. I did already know the song when I had my Near Death Experience, and it was part of my daily practice at that time.

The form of the Song of the Vajra on paper, as it was given to me, looked like an explosion to me, when I saw it. My previous life flashed back to me. It reminded me of my previous life and journey through the death bardo. It was the same as the form I decided my poetry should take. Some have also indicated that they think it looks like an indestructible *vajra,* when shown in this way. A vajra is a ritual item symbolizing a thunderbolt or diamond. So, this is a bit of a secret element of why it was so important for me to write the poems in this way.

The Song of the Vajra appeared in the same way that the explosion from the end of my last lifetime had suddenly appeared. That sudden violent boom had delivered me to this lifetime, surrounded by song, in an incredible explosion of the inexplicable. The sounds of the poetry I then created also made sense, when written in this way, centered in the form of an explosive cloud rising into the sky, larger poetic devices leading to more specific elements, trailing to nothing, compression, release, intensity, then light. It is not a mistake that the poetry of this Luminous Mala has a strong visual quality, which accompanies the natural sounds and rhythm of each note. It is much like anything else, the clouds provide the meaning and structure within space. Conversely, space is inexpressible, unobtainable, often ignored, holding the true meaning for all that we perceive.

I feel very fortunate to have met so many amazing teachers, and to have been prepared by them to meet death. I have taken the elements of disaster and transformed that. Without having received teachings and integrated all of that into my daily life, there would have been no possibility that I could have remembered or explored this form of poetry through deep contemplation. So many amazing teachers are available in our current age, so many opportunities are available for us to receive help in awakening, that it is surprising to me that everyone has not been helped in some way, or sought out teachers who could help. What seems to be lacking is a more contemporary context for this, one where we can integrate in a practical way, without spending many years learning about complex teachings, and techniques of practice, which involve cultural elements that we cannot fathom. Hopefully, this work cuts through all of that to the most basic elements, so that we can all access what we have always known.

Please enjoy. Do not take any of this too seriously, and don't take my word for it. Examine your mind, look inwardly to see what awaits. Relax.

See that what I have created is really just a contemplation of the immutable. It's not really about death, it's about our amazing potentiality that we experience very clearly, when we die. It's about living with that potentiality, discovering timeless luminosity.

Listen without narrative, just as it is, so that you may hear. Say it out loud or quietly to yourself, only in your mind. Or, better yet, sing the words to a spontaneous melody. Take your time, savor the words, relax, slow down. When you are done with that, listen again.

Blessings,

Bob

TIMELESS LUMINOSITY

The very first teaching
was
Dzogchen,
long before we had
physical presence,
long before there were stars,
or the formation of planets,
long before the explosive beginning
of this universe, or the one before it,
or before that, or even before that
through timeless beginnings and endings;
Dzogchen is timeless, originating
from primordial nature of mind,
luminous, with greater intensity than
all of the universe combined,
or even a million universes all at once,
or even every universe there has ever been;
It is luminous beyond all fabricated thoughts,
well beyond ordinary human perception;
Dzogchen is beyond all constraints,
beyond any potentiality
we think we may have,
beyond concept and reason,
or any idea;

AH

Dzogchen is
spacious conscious awareness,
empty cognizance,
Dharmakaya itself;

The primordial Buddha,
the first teacher,
Samantabhadra,
who came from beginningless beginnings,
who was not a being as we know beings to be,
is pure wisdom consciousness, empty awareness,
ultimate luminous compassion, bright light
all-good now perfection, perfect luminosity,
the primordial Buddha of Dharmakaya,
teaching that most perfect teaching
luminous beyond all luminosity,

the root of all Buddhas,
resting in that natural state, resting now
in that pure empty cognizance, beyond time,
that all-good awareness of this moment;

Dzogchen was always there, present
in the ever-luminous unborn wonder
of timeless Dharmakaya, beyond thought,
beyond all extremes and limitations;

With each Buddha, appearing as pure energy, lightness,
energetic sound, rays of color streaming in a realm
beyond our physical manifestation as we know it,
Dzogchen appeared in teaching form, at some point,
relating to the dimension of Sambhogakaya;
Beings of pure energy and light, would become
amazed at this display of pure wisdom
emanating from timeless luminosity,
vibrations so much brighter than light;

AH
As it is;

When a Buddha would
appear in a physical dimension,
as Nirmanakaya Buddha,
observable by ordinary beings,
so, too, would Dzogchen appear in some way,
at some point,
revealing itself perfectly
when beings would be ready to hear it,
when they had evolved sufficiently enough
to remember the ever-present
original primordial teachings
that have been a part of all beings,
since beginningless time,
which continue to be a part of us all
in this instant of nowness, even though
we may be distracted and obsess about this or that,
the magical display of mind, ignorantly finding ourselves
trapped in a cycle of our own making, suffering,
not knowing that we are simply, perplexingly,
an emanation of the Dharmakaya as well,
not knowing what this Nirmanakaya is,
this physical illusory dimension of dream-like magic,

emanating timelessly from pure wisdom,
ultimate love and compassion, bodhicitta;

Ordinary beings fret about this teaching and
that teaching, not knowing what to believe,
saying, "Oh, Dzogchen is only a few centuries old,
so, it is just another teaching," or "Wait, it was also
there a few thousand years before that with
another Buddha," or "What about before that?
Is it not said that there are infinite Buddhas,
beginning with the primordial Buddha? Is it
also not said that time is possibly just
beginningless, or an illusion?
What about all these other teachings?"
or, "I have heard these teachings are found
on other planets as well, maybe thirteen
world systems, or more, or many more,
maybe all world systems have teachings,
trillions upon trillions of them,
all across multi-universes, too many
to fathom, some people believe that;"
Believe nothing!
It will only lead to ruin;
The primordial teachings are not belief, they
are direct experience of primordial wisdom!
They are not teachings of useless beliefs!
These teachings are ever-present and have always
been ever-present in this eternal now;

Timeless luminosity is not outside yourself,
and it is not constrained by our limitations,
and notions of life, death, space and time!
Such knowledge cannot have a beginning,
it cannot have a place;
Stop your fretting!

Primordial wisdom,
which is timeless luminosity, seen at death,
is beyond concept, has no beginning and no end,
it is as it is, beyond all;
Do not trust your limited view!
If you must believe something,
then only temporarily believe,
due to simply not being ready
for that knowledge;

Use your own ignorance as a tool
for awakening,
use compassionate wisdom
as a guide,
forming only useful beliefs, due to your own oblivion,
compassionate towards your own ignorant state,
with the notion that any belief must be
cast aside as something completely useless,
at some point, as you change,
as your capacity increases;

The Buddha, Buddha Shakyamuni taught this!
At some point, as your heart opens up, and
your capacity increases in that way,
you will know when you are ready to
seek teachings that will help, and
seek teachings everywhere, gathering them up
for the useful purpose of awakening;

Begin by simply knowing that this all
is just an illusion, a dream from which you
have not been able to awaken, and are not able
to remain at ease, as you would like;
So, simply seek teachings of Buddha, a being
of awareness, a being who can be seen only
with your heart, not your created ideas,
someone closer to you than you can imagine;
When you see Buddha, you see luminosity,
you see great compassion, you see unlimited
love and wisdom, timelessly manifesting
in our limited physical reality;

Buddha Shakyamuni, the Buddha of our time,
began teaching in the physical dimension,
then he taught in the energetic dimension,
then he manifested in the primordial dimension;
Practice those teachings inwardly,
emanate those teachings outwardly,
increase your capacity secretly;
If you persist, remaining diligent,
compassionate towards yourself
in all ways possible, persevering
in your practice of mind, you
will awaken, the Dharmakaya
will, once again, manifest

within your entire presence of life,
your empty cognizance will become all-pervasive
in every moment of this magical display,
through awareness of your physical condition,
through awareness of your energy aspects,
through awareness of your primordial wisdom;

AH

Here at last that one taste of our real nature, beyond suffering,
that spacious consciousness of wisdom awareness
has arisen in every moment;
See it all as it is, just let it be,
rest in that primordial wisdom, be present
in that luminous state of our real nature
that we all know so well, but have forgotten;

You are Buddha.

OM
AH
HUM

DHARMAKAYA GURU

Beyond,
listen within that
unborn state
of being,
listen, see, feel,
as unchanging tides of mind
radiate to unborn shores,
beyond all senses,
from infinite luminosity,
unseen reflections, luminous clarity
beyond knowing,
beyond being,
now
without obscurations, present
in that magnificent source
of all-knowing immutable
clarity,
we see that this is not separate,
that is not one apart,

nor many unified, nor that scattered,
simply being as it is, simply being
simply that presence that is
that beyond that
which we know through
direct experience, directly encountering
timeless luminosity in all its splendor
of mind, instantly present
in our primordial
condition;
All manifestations, all beyond
that appears as
Dharmakaya,
infinite beyond realization, beyond thought,
all that bright condition in this
eternal moment, all that is
guru of our real condition,
beyond, far beyond all that is,
inseparable, seen only with unlimited capacity
meeting this guru only then, though
you have never been separate, seeing
without reification, without something there,
just being in that, of that perfect nature of mind
that natural state beyond
beyond any possibility
within any possibility or notion of limits
beyond confusion or distress,
relaxed, aware,
simply abiding within
that overwhelming
luminous perfect contemplation
perfection beyond all,
with infinite potententiality,
like a mirror reflecting
bright, beyond bright
intensity brilliance
unchanging,
without
beginning,
without
end.

SAMBHOGAKAYA GURU

Energy emerging from that ineffable
radiance beyond, timelessly perfect bright space,
within, beyond, neither beyond
nor within, nor outside, yet both, pervasive
cognizance, indescribable
turbulent swirling rays of light,
bright colors manifesting
without substance, song without self
in the realm of Buddhas and Bodhisattvas,
manifesting as pure energetic
delight, enjoyment body of light
Sambhogakaya
bliss
light laughter
radiance of present awareness
its cognizant nature
ground, from emptiness, pure enjoyment,
out of pure light Dharmakaya,
timeless, luminous, unchanging
suchness, empty then suddenly
vividly swirling eddies, cyclones of light,
look where energy now manifests
motion as light of apparent
cognizance;
This energy looks at the Nirmanakaya
manifestation, delighting in beings who wonder
and wander, seeing what is happening
before there is this delusion
of self appearing, this embodiment
that appears to senses forming,
it is the rushing of winds,
the energy
of color,
the essence
of form,
manifesting as cognizance,
itself dynamic
perceptive,
passing through
kinetic quantum
knowing,
motion
of knowing beyond

without
self
appearing.

NIRMANAKAYA GURU

Appearing
as physical manifestations,
the union
of emptiness and cognizance
dance before our senses
in magical union;
Where cognizance and emptiness appear,
this physical body remains
as enlightenment,
suffused with joy,
ineffable radiance, a physical body, knowing
this illusion appears real;
Our own guru,
having been our guru, becoming
our own guru,
in a timeless display of primordial wisdom,
where even our own delusions
spring forth from ultimate bodhicitta,
from ultimate compassion,
from ultimate wisdom,
with sublime radiance,
that cannot be measured,
like space, timeless in this
infinite now;
We see
Nirmanakaya
manifesting here
at this
moment
that cannot be
named
conceptualized,
nor reified,
indescribable
in
this now
moment.

1

Careless Beings!
Watch this fixation unfold!
This dream is none other than mind's illusion,
appearing in this moment;
Do not fixate on any of it!
Awaken to your true nature
in that space before the story can be told;
Drop all labels into the vast empty void,
remain completely relaxed,
without words or thoughts remaining;
See that reality which defies explanation,
as it truly is, in its naked state,
without fabricating anything;
Are you awake?
Let that go before you answer;
Are you asleep?
Let that go as well;
See clearly
that this life
is nothing other
than a dream,
a dream within illusion
emerging from light;
See clearly
that
dreams
are not different
than daily
life.

2

HRIH!
HRIH!
HRIH!

If you glimpse but a little
of this great magical display
playing before your eyes, your senses,
where you see this potentiality of being able
able to be just a little bit happy,
capable of relieving all suffering,
transforming this dream into anything,
with unlimited possibilities,
seeing that it is completely possible
to awaken to our real condition,
then drift no more!
If you do not seek
happiness, or
if compassion
means nothing
to you, then go back
go back as you were,
as you drift helplessly
in this ocean of suffering;
If the spark of kindness has not
been ignited in your being, then
wait for another opportunity
in the eons to come;
Time is an illusion,
along with your
suffering;
It is
up to you,
you alone,
this miracle is
just
as simple
as
that.

3

Listen!

Echoes of time in this present moment
the distant past and future, presently
surrounding this great illusion
of just what we think
is happening,
listen;

Be at peace now,
listen now,
be aware
now,
it could be
as you think it might be,
or it might be
beyond such busy nonsense;

Listen to what is happening
inside this moment unfolding
appearing disappearing
now;

What is that?

Just listen!

4

Beings who slumber
cannot see their guru who
is screaming for them to awaken;
The energy builds as he screams,
BUDDHA, RENOUNCE THIS SLEEP!
He screams with all his might, he
SCREAMS, SCREAMS SCREAMS!
"No no not now" say beings, "We
want peace and deep sleep.
We want peaceful dreams,
go away guru, you are
disturbing the peace."
And so, they sleep
and they slumber,
they snore,
they fart,
and

5

This ocean,
where suffering manifests
in waves of random discontent,
where even what we think
we want
brings just more of the same
misery, unbearable pain,
and we find ourselves buffeted,
drifting aimlessly,
unable to escape
or find safety for even a moment,
at the mercy of storms and
great terrors of the deep,
oh, what can be done?

What will stop this endless pain,
this anxiety, this unreliableness,
this insanity?

Truly, nothing of the mind
arises
without cause
without warning,
truly
this is mind,
as it drifts
aimlessly
in the ocean
of
suffering.

6

Luminosity, unchanging, beyond
beyond ordinary understanding,
beyond, beyond
that which we talk about,
where there is no
where, there is no there
beyond empty white, beyond
extreme bright,
we are not separate from
that immeasurable
presence,
timelessly perfect,
eternal,
that which we
see upon dying,
again
and again,
perfect wisdom,
perfect
from the beginning,
from before
beginningless beginnings,
as it has
always been,
as
it
is
now.

7

AH

It is here in this place which has no substance,
swirling in this manifestation of insubstantial
pure mind,
that I take ultimate refuge, irreversible,
with dynamic energy;

HUM! HUM! HUM!

All the world is but a dream
within a dream,
within a dream,
within dreams unending,
unlimited wisdom folding into
this moment of pure joy;

HO! HO! HO!

Now I see this expanse,
and it is empty;

OM AH HUM

It is time to be
just that
moment
luminous
insubstantial
everything
beyond
all beyond
imagination

AH

AH

AH

8

Morning's walk at sunrise
appears endless,
seeing that bright light
just there beyond,
illuminated within stillness, as I breathe slowly,
wandering amid vast appearances,
contemplations beyond thought,
radiating in this simple moment,
the next moment, the next
this endless moment that cannot be described,
where each step sounds gently
amid this growing chorus of sunrise creatures
in forest and swamp, a splash, a ripple, rustling,
silence then chirping, singing with joy, wing beats,
becoming rainbow colors,
magnificently appearing energy
of light and rays and sound,
where all simply is
as it is;
Perfection.

9

Oh, to see that subtle bloom,
timeless bright luminosity
arising moment by moment,
as each deliberate step,
passing by, and gone,
awakens this darkened forest
from ancient slumber;

AH

What further radiance
awaits?

10

Listening to rain
we are asked to believe,
believe that that is real, though it is illusion;
More important than that,
know what that really is;
Each drop falling,
listening to that,
it is not nearly enough to merely listen,
be aware that you are listening
to each drop
each drop falling;
Being mindful
of that magical appearance,
that apparition, it is not nearly enough
to be merely mindful
of that,
be aware that you are being
mindful,
be present in that;
Being aware,
with an open heart,
it is not nearly enough
to simply know,
know the essence of everything;
Be aware of being aware,
realize the nature of all
awareness;
In this moment,
listening to rain,
being
mindful of rain,
being
aware of self
listening to rain,
knowing this
awareness,
this presence of mind,
being aware of
awareness,
that
is appearing as a most

precious
magical display
of mind
always
forever
now.

11

Though horizons vanish without a trace,
our supreme moment remains
undisturbed
as reflections past carry us
without moving, without
stirring;
Turbulence, turmoil, storms tossing us about,
explosive dynamics, quantum
expansion, contraction, disappearances,
appearances of mind going on forever,
super-cyclones dancing in our mind,
wormholes of delusion and dread
sending us into unknown terror
fractious wayward chaos
spinning our senses
into discord,
when we
breathe
relax
in
that,
relax, just relax,
and let clarity arise,
that ever-bright moment
we know so well
is always
just there
here
now,
just relax
see
what is
clarity.

12

AH

Resting in the simplicity of our natural state,
that nondual indescribable moment,
our real condition where we meet
we meet when death
illuminates
beyond conventional
understanding,
in the body of light,
in the body of energy,
in this body,
this mind
of non-discriminatory
awareness;

OM AH HUM!

OM AH HUM!

OM AH HUM!

13

That inexpressible,
ineffable
luminous
AH
relaxed
in that authentic
state of being,
that
that
that
wondrous now
that has no form
no boundary, no center,
quiescence beyond
imagination

that
song beyond singing
moving indistinguishably from any
thing, time, or place,
that
that
everything nothing
not nothing not everything
where there is not a self to know
and yet it is known
absolutely,
in that state without motion
energy emerges without
emergence,
seeing that
physical manifestation through
consciousness
mantras and mudras emerge
bringing that physical body into being
where consciousness dynamics
converge with empty all,
and in this state, the body comes into being,
as this awakened state magically
becomes what it
already
always
has
been.

14

Look
at this moment
look at the moment before that
and before that, and
just what is happening here?
I can't remember,
it goes on and on
in this eternal perfect moment,
and before that,
that that that
that moment, that
thought of me drifting

throughout eternity
without any idea what is happening,
none, no idea, none
none whatsoever, just
drifting though suffering unending
this
moment
this
time of
reflecting, this stream of moments;
I want to get off this cosmic rollercoaster ride;
I want an end to all the pain,
the suffering that
I cannot escape,
this moment,
this horrible
eternal life
this delusion that I feel
that I know only too well;
Now is the time,
now is the time
to do something about it,
now is the time to awaken,
awaken to that timeless bright condition
before my life is completed
and another has started,
before I forget
again,
and,
again
and again
and
and
and

15

Inside this moment
inside this body
inside this mind,
all that appears cannot be known
all that we perceive is illusion
the knower and the knowing

cannot be found, we see
we see those approaching
who will decide through ignorance
or insanity, with repulsion
or desire,
those who wander confused
not knowing, not known, neither the knower
nor the found,
anguishing,
tense,
judging,
they are not out there,
they are inside
this mad wreck
this ancient apparition
this insane manifestation
this, this
moment
inside.

16

Luminosity, unchanging,
beyond
beyond ordinary understanding,
beyond
beyond that which we talk about,
where there is no
where,
beyond bright white, beyond
beyond our understanding of brightness;
We are not separate from
that immeasurable
infinite presence, that knowing
that unfathomable knowing
that beyond time
beyond light
beyond
wisdom;
We are
timeless luminosity.

17

Consciousness,
empty cognizance
within empty space,
bright luminous, beyond time
conscious
of
colors
of
sound
of energy
of
movement,
this simple knowing,
present only now, now
now
in this waking moment
where there is no movement
where luminosity fills us
with so much enjoyment
that we cannot fully
grasp, grasp
this motion
until
until we
form
an idea of just what
this might be,
realizing
realizing that
it cannot
cannot
be
grasped,
we know
we
must
rest.

18

In this moment
of clarity, we see
the key to happiness,
as if appearing from pure light;

We see that suffering exists,
and that it has a cause;
We see clearly that a path exists
away from suffering,
and that this path is one of
most excellent
presence
of mind
and virtue;

Can anything
bring
happiness
that is
more
pure
than
this?

19

purify

just purify

THIS WANDERING CORPSE STINKS!

purify this wandering mess
this mind stinks as well
these emotions stink
purify at once

purify or it will be too late
purify or really
this corpse will become just another
corpse
this mind will think it is
someone else
forgetting that
it
must
purify
this state of being
this empty cognizant moment

IN THIS MOMENT!

while there is still time

purify
now

20

Examine this life,
see that self that we create, that
cannot be located;
See that self, see that
it is your own creation;
See that you
you defend with your life,
your ego, your self;
If
if you can see
the immaterial nature
of this life, this self, this illusion
that which you hold so dear,
then it is easy, oh so easy
easy to see what will happen next
when all changes, when everything is different;
As our consciousness
transmigrates, transmigrates through moments
from life to death to that next life, even in this life,
it keeps doing the same, transmigrating
between moments, it transmigrates, as it goes on

changing, fabricating, creating, inventing
this idea of self,
working so hard to fabricate
that which continuously appears
appears to all the senses,
which are oh-so-pathetically-limited;
If this consciousness transmigrates
through the winds of karma,
through uncertain oceans of suffering,
transmigrates through moments
moments without awakening,
then the cycle begins
begins again;
We are reborn
in a new life, just as
every moment of every life
in every moment of this life
every moment becomes a new life;
It's not this self that begins again
again, through cyclic existence,
this self doesn't begin again,
it's not a new self, because
self never existed, it is
awareness
in each moment
appearing as delusion,
it is delusion,
this fabrication
we call
self.

21

Grasping
at this illusion
this fluttering stream
of now changing,
swirling in the ebb,
flashing in
void-riddled space,
energy fields of pure
colors, rays of light, song, churning
moments that seem to go on forever

swirling eddies of delusion,
we pretend that it is real,
we convince ourselves
that
this
dream
has substance;
How can
we
be so stupid?

22

Distractions, obstacles, pain
appearing, falling into our lives,
seemingly from nowhere, out of nothing,
creating havoc that we cling to,
that we grasp very tightly,
where we find ourselves
obsessing about that,
how can it be?
We
are not that, we are not that;
We
find ourselves,
we discover being
in that state of suffering
without
without even thinking about that;
We
find that we
cannot loosen our grip,
cannot change our gaze,
cannot let ourselves fall
cannot open our heart, to what may be
though we know that
we know that, we know
that is what we must
do;
It is
so simple
to
just

let
it
all
go.

23

This breath,
this breath never leaves
us when we are alive,
this breath we must breathe
we must breathe;
Breathe this breath,
be at peace
in this breath,
see only this breath,
breathe,
breathe breath,
be at peace in this breath,
just relax
in that
breath
of
life.

24

When we relax
we find peace,
which is very
simple
to know;
We find peace when we relax;
This is very obvious
and, yet, it eludes us;
Without peace, we cannot find
truth,
by looking or by
any other means;
We cannot find
what

actually
is
is
is
is
is
in this moment
now.

25

Who
can have faith everlasting
without examining
phenomena?
Belief, without examination,
inner reflection, of belief
is just arbitrary nonsense;
Appearances must be examined
carefully, studied, debated
questioned, scrutinized, observed,
run through the mill of logic and experience,
or there can be no faith that will last;
Even when we think we know,
we do not
know,
it is all just that
strange
magical illusion
dancing in our mind,
in our mind where we tear it all down,
those worthless beliefs
in our mind, ideas dancing,
shouting that they want to be made real,
recognized, rationalized, reified
gentrified, deified
solidified
aggrandized
in an unnecessarily complex
nonsensical illusion of hope and fear,
promising to make us comforted;
Going down this, that crazy mad
rabbit hole of all rabbit holes;

we see that none of it, none
of it can ever be located,
and, in not locating,
we begin
to understand
mind;
In so doing
we are
discovering real faith,
great confidence,
slowly, slowly, we discover
primordial nature,
the nature
of mind's own wisdom,
faith in our real potential, as
Buddha.

26

What is this gap
between
death and death?
Look at that turbulent turmoil
that excruciating
scattering, explosive, crushing
complication
that
fixation where we cannot focus
that
insanity that has been our passion
since beginningless beginnings
we have been thinking it is real
thinking
thinking
that that
that gap has
some relevance
something different
from our eternal
awakened state
that awakening that
we can barely remember
from that flash of infinite wisdom

ultimate wisdom unending;
What is that?
That becoming without becoming,
that brightness beyond belief, a dream
fabricated within a dream
within a dream,
within
a dream,
where was that?
Is it beyond where we are now?
What was that?
What
is
going
on
here
?

27

We
have ourselves
to blame
for not understanding
for not realizing
these forms
sensations
feelings
that appear before
our eyes
with sound
what we smell and feel
with our bodies and mind
these physical attributes
of being alive,
we come to the wrong
conclusions,
about that,
we think it is something
substantial,
something relevant,
something

real.
Our senses ignore
ultimate reality, that timeless luminosity
because our senses cannot
perceive what is really
happening,
they cannot
they cannot,
and so
we
we wander in this delusion,
through our actions, based on ignorance,
consciously giving name to these formations,
craving
more of it, grasping, becoming,
becoming reborn in this life once again,
a person of discontent, becoming ill and aging
until we die
and we repeat
consciously repeat
repeat
forevermore, until we
awaken
from
that uneasy
dream.

28

This life
seemingly useless
this life
so far from death,
seemingly removed from that timeless luminous
state of being that we experience in death
this life, this jumbled confusion,
we crave to return
to that pristine place of natural being
home, that place we imagine is far,
so far away, that primordial condition,
that that that

whatever that is
that state of being we know when
we are in the light,
at death,
during our death experience,
and we don't know
why;
Why should we find
ourselves
in this condition of anxious life?
We don't know why
we should have such a
precious life.

THAT IS ALL RUBBISH!

We have this magical
precious life,
as we know full-well,
deep down we know
we know very well that we have this life
so that we can use our lives
in amazing ways,
to find our
way back, no matter what,
despite all setbacks,
despite terrible suffering,
through love, as if it were a miracle,
through great compassion
to that awakened state;
That is what makes
our lives
so very
precious
rare
and
magical.

29

Look at mind,
just look
don't take it in in such a way that it takes over,
just look at that, if you can
relax
observe that this mind has no substance
it cannot be located,
don't worry if you can't see it
nobody
can see that
that phantom that
obsessionary bundle of labels
worries, distracting reflections
anxiety, laughter, obnoxious
assertions, assumptions, appearances, fabrications
place holders in a reality that never stays the same,
never stays the same for even a moment
just look at that
that that that that that;
What is that?
Where is that?
When is that?
How is that?
Why is that?
Just keep looking
just look, and relax when you look
don't worry about hallucinations
don't worry about
demons
don't worry about
all those obsessions, those things bumping around
those things that cannot be explained,
just look at mind, without flinching, without batting an eyelash,
with perseverance, with
with
with
with,
with courage.

30

Beginning
must begin
with pure intention,
with that knowledge
that one must
awaken
perfectly awaken
beyond all notions
of awakening,
one must,
with pure heart,
sincerely
wish
to go beyond
to do whatever it takes
to confront all that stands in the way
to be willing to open your heart
and mind
completely
without fear
without holding anything back without
without
without the slightest hesitation or worry about protecting oneself
from all those demons we must face
from friends who quickly turn to enemies
from family who quickly attack our most sensitive
places of the heart,
for simply not
agreeing
to continue
in that
eternal
confusion, that
suffering
that
that that pain without end;
We must
definitely decide
upon purity with
this intention
to go

beyond into
pure
light.

31

All this jumbled mess
in our heads
in our distracted messy minds
bouncing around, flinging shit at things,
imaginary monkeys
looking here and over by that thing
that thing you cannot get out of your mind,
that thing you won't stop fixating upon
that thing all covered in shit, that
that mess you produce everywhere you go
everywhere you go with your mind looking
at that thing
over there, over here
that thing, that mess
all covered in all that shit
that that shit you seem to be okay
with just letting it be, covered
that way, smelling up your day,
all that shit you hurl, as if
as if it were okay, okay
ooh, ooh oh, okay
with just letting that stench stinking it all up
perpetually stifling
your senses,
stuffed right up your nose, filling that,
orifice of inner perception, that
that shit you should have taken care of long ago, long before you
started jumping around looking at everything
in your mind, staying distracted by that,
fixating on everything except what is important,
those people laughing at purity, laughing at cleaning up all this shit,
they're all shit! don't listen to them
clean up this dirty stinkin' smelly conglomerate
of a jumbled mess you have created;
It's your mess, clean it up!
Think about that, fixate on how it will be once

once it is clean, so clean that
you can relax
relax
get busy cleaning all this
stuff,
it's
important,
it's important if you,
if you wish
to awaken,
becoming
light.

32

many who seek awakening
will not be able to open
will not have capacity
will not seek it
for the right
reason

33

This idea of reincarnation
this idea of being the same person reborn
from lifetime to lifetime
this whole idea that one person holds together,
keeping personhood alive,
is rather stupid;
There is nothing to say
that you can't be
reborn, reborn reborn
as two, or twelve,
as a hundred
or a thousand
or a hundred thousand
individuals,
as your consciousness,

TIMELESS LUMINOSITY

your awakened potentiality
is just energy, and not even that,
it can be split, or combined,
scattered, disseminated, crushed, dispersed,
or condensed into one again;
Here we are, flying through the gap that is death,
becoming integrated with timeless luminosity
entering the many states
of luminous experience, becoming
becoming that next being, whatever it will be,
having forgotten completely,
forgotten where we had been;
It's stupid, really,
we're not who we think we are;
It's not you that comes back,
it can't be, you never really existed;
Who is this?
Who is this person who
that is totally back from the stream
in the stream, that glorious
stream?
It's a stream of consciousness
flowing
ebbing flowing
through our our
OUR
real condition in that
that beyond us thatness that
timeless luminosity
that we see at death, before
before that consciousness
sees
sees another being magically appearing
from that, that that we sometimes
remember;
We cease to be that
dream we had invented
rather becoming what we
always had been, luminous
timelessly luminous and perfect,
that inexplicable amazing expanse,
our bright primordial state beyond
beyond enlightened thoughts
being beyond all thought
our

real
nature;
Then something else,
sometimes many, sometimes few,
someone
else
returns from
that.

34

This death we are about to face
it's there, just there
in this next moment
or out beyond in a few years,
it's lurking just there, not too far away,
whether we want it to or not
or not not, with time not known, without choice,
this uncertainty that is always just there,
this death is bound to happen
at some point, it will happen,
we will all be forced to face
timeless luminosity
and this amazing gap between lives,
we will face that certainty
once again, death,
it will happen,
appearing not separate
not separate from this self,
this fictitious thing we think we are,
this self-person we have created
just as it has always happened
again, again
and again, and again and again
from beginningless beginnings,
beginnings buried deeply in our mind,
those many lifetimes
that were not really beginnings;
Look at that unreality
that is death, that is life,
that is life and rebirth and dreams;
That is this cyclone carrying us,
that thing we see so clearly,

without really wanting to see
that
that thing we don't see at all,
that spinning momentary cyclic existence,
that thing that is not a thing,
that thing that is not real,
that thing, death, that is just a gap,
where we become
open
to infinite possibilities,
and, yet, it is inevitable, as inevitable
as our life, our life, which is not separate
not separate from that other life, that other death;
Look at that inseparability, that symbiosis, contemplate
what it is you must go through
that gap called death
that is not there,
where the only thing you carry
is that, that
which is in your mind,
which is mind, and then
it all dissolves
dissolving into that pool of ancient wisdom,
brighter than all lights in the universe,
brighter than a billion universes
all light everywhere, all at once, through the quantum
where there is no difference between you and other,
where another being appears to your mind,
another being appears, reappearing again, again
that being that connects to your essence,
though it is not you, it is something new, it is
resulting your actions
your consciousness transmigrating,
grasping, clinging to this life,
that life, and all those demons
that you brought with you, all that;
Are you ready for that?!
THAT?!!!?
For that which is carried with mind,
by mind, must be faced,
for it will determine the next life
and the next
and, and
every life that appears
will be carried

from the last thought
to the next, for all eternity,
all that baggage
held by empty cognizance
that noisy terrifying shocking
overpowering
stuff you carry
must be faced, not by choice,
because of not knowing,
because of actions,
all that
must be faced;
Timeless luminosity,
Dharmakaya,
that which liberates us
must be
experienced
directly, if we
wish
to
escape.

35

Mind, looking
at mind, at mind,
in that reflective
matrix without end
that
infinitely repeating
appearance
of nothing that can be located
by anyone,
just look
look at that,
at that condition that causes so much
bluster,
so much bother in one's life,
look at that before
death
comes
to
you.

36

These wounds run deep
these wounds we cling to, that we hold,
these injuries we hold precious,
that we
keep, guard, protect
as if a rare jewel
as if, as if
a unique gem had been formed
formed in that pain of our heart
formed deep down amid tectonic fissures
that now violently exploding from a nuclear core
in a flash of intense crushing thunderous burning
expanding outward in a steady stream
of injury, pain and anger,
as if it were, as if it was,
as if, as if
it never
was
that;
And just why is that?
This wound, these wounds,
have
no purpose
whatsoever, they are not real,
not real, not real in the least, beyond
beyond appearances that we hold;
We find no one looking
we find nothing there
but thine own
mind.

37

Enlightenment
is not so very serious,
once you realize you
are dreaming this dream,
this illusion within a dream
a very hard dream

called daily life;
See that
you,
the you whom you cannot find,
that fabricated opinionated
dream notion
of self, that self
will awaken within
that dream
within a dream, within
within an endless stream of dreams,
this continuous illusion,
of life and death and rebirth
and constant dreaming,
within
within that dream
you
keep
thinking
is real.

HA HA HA,
HA
HO!

HO!

HO!!

HO!!!!

38

This real condition,
this illusion within the light of death,
this cognizant spatial timeless brightness,
awareness beyond reason, beyond thought,
infinite brightness beyond any light,
this all surrounding, this all-good,
this pervasive primordial wisdom
ultimate compassion
seemingly ephemeral
phenomenal appearances

that dance before our senses,
within that, within
that bright light, timelessly perfect,
Dharmakaya
eludes our ordinary mind
even though
it
is
all there is
and all
that is beyond
all there is
beyond any fixation
or idea
beyond
thought
with infinite
potential, infinite possibilities
that timeless luminosity
eludes our limited mind,
our physical condition,
keeping us deluded
keeping us feeling
separated
from those
infinite
possibilities.

39

Relax, just relax,
you have absolutely nothing to worry about
nothing to
see outside
yourself,
just relax in that infinite light
beyond self, encompassing self
within indestructability
timelessly within
this moment
that seems so real,
this infinite wisdom
that seems to elude

us all,
though that is always present
always present
in this infinite moment
where we spend all our time
fretting
suffering
angsting,
feeling like nothing is ever quite right
no matter
what,
no matter whatever happens,
just relax,
relax,
it's not out there
it's in here,
everything,
everything you need,
and that which is beyond,
everything
is
within
us.

40

I began
by lucid dreaming,
being aware that I was
dreaming,
dreaming dreaming
every moment dreaming
being aware of that dream
that spills into daily life,
a very big heavy dream
that I remember
more clearly than
the rest;
I began that way;
I began that way dreaming,
not with birth
not thinking of rebirth,
not with death, I began

dreaming, just dreaming,
remembering that dream from
one day to the next
sometimes at night, I would remember,
and then I remembered
before that, this dream,
this endless stream of dreams unfolding in this eternal moment,
this moment of quiet solitude, within my mind,
dreaming my day away, dreaming my night,
just dreaming that way,
then practicing to be aware
in that dream
looking
at mind,
in that way
I began,
aware of this awareness now,
which cannot be located,
empty of any sort of substance,
cognizantly aware
of this illusion
unfolding
now.

41

We can examine
this life,
see what it is that is
just what is going on here,
see our body continually changing,
see our thoughts changing,
continually changing,
see the world around us
continually changing,
see this idea of self continually
changing,
see that
nothing remains the same
for more than a
moment,
and not even that,
not even

that;
Sameness
is an illusion,
separateness
an illusion,
this life, an illusion,
everything is passing us by
in this dream that is not as we think it is
impermanent, insubstantial
inconclusive
intangible, indescribable
illusory
in a way that is easily not there,
passing on by
at great speed,
precious and rare
though
not
really
this or that,
not really
anything
at
all.

42

People scoff
at virtue,
thinking
this does not apply
to them,
thinking
they can do whatever they want
it won't matter
it doesn't make
a difference,
that people won't have an issue with that,
thinking
their life will be more happy
that way, just being on a rampage of selfish insanity;
Such nonsense!
Of course, everything

you do
makes all the difference,
everything we do
leads to that same condition
we all find ourselves in, that
that frustration, that anxiety, that unsatisfactory destruction,
it should be plainly evident that we cannot
ignorantly proceed
without understanding
this key point,
that nothing at all
anywhere
can exist
without everything else also existing, because of that,
existing even though it is also just passing us by,
just an illusion dreamt within a dream
and we affect all of that,
our virtue, or nonvirtue, makes everything that, our action;
If we proceed causing harm, acting in this way
through nonvirtue,
we cause harm everywhere
we cause problems for ourselves, even if
we think
we are alone.
It is said that kindness
attracts
kindness;
Why
did
you
not
know
that?

43

That
is nothing
whatsoever,
though not
nothing, nor not
not nothing;
Our thoughts,

our senses, our fixation
all lead us to the mistaken notion
that that is something;
How can it be something?
It doesn't
'happen'
for more than a
moment;
All this crazy whacky unbelievable
'stuff'
that we think is real
was never really there;
Only our fixation and
nonsensical ideas
give it
'form';
In our mind, we give that form,
an ephemeral label arises
out of emptiness
we
'pretend'
that it is
'real'
we just pretend;
In reality,
if there is such a thing as that,
that is not to be located,
not to be found
without applying
some sort of label, and even then
it is not really there,
it is not to be found
beyond
its essence;
It is empty of all
substantiality,
an empty cognizance,
appearances through senses,
that's
all.

44

When we look at
'our self'
through inner reflection,
through deep contemplation,
looking into that mirror
of our real nature,
looking deeply
to where
we see
that
illusion,
that fiction we create
for ourself, of ourself, no one else,
so much this and that, jumbled overwhelming agitation,
this self that does not exist, that energetic
'happening'
of mind cognizing what seems to appear
reflecting upon our real condition getting in
touch with this personhood reflecting
its primordial nature, its
real condition of emptiness;
we see infinite possibilities,
we see that we
ourself can create
whatever it wants to create;
we create our place in the cosmos, our definitions of what it all means,
we create that in the mirror of our real being,
we create a world
and a place in the world, cosmos, universe,
so much good stuff, we create it all from our place of being
ignorantly grasping
we create all of that
all that confused
nonsense;
keep looking
at mind,
see that it does not exist in any substantial way,
see that all that
'stuff'
is just
an illusion that could be anything

any possibility could
arise
in that.

45

each action
every action
causes
suffering
each action causes,
creates, attachment to
that most sinister idea of
of causing more actions,
harmful actions, to happen;
there is no end to this
karmic action and actions of
of response of reactions of
grasping to that cause
of more actions of
of of acting on
the perceived notions that you must act
that you must send these ripples into time
that that you must cause others to become fixated on, on suffering
and the perpetuation of suffering and reacting to suffering,
becoming bound to the actions which created the suffering, which
which create more suffering and an escalation of suffering off
off into the cosmos for eons to come;
what is that nonsense, that senseless meaningless two-bit crazy
hornet's nest of desire, of hatred, of ignoring what this really means?
this butterfly effect is something you stir up,
you stir this up with your actions, everything
you do stirs all this up, creating
actions and reactions
that go on forever
spreading suffering
throughout
all time
in all directions
in this delusion
of
mind.

46

If you wish to go
where you want to go
from one lifetime to
another,
there is no other way than to
train the mind,
no other way!
But that doesn't matter,
awakening
matters;
Freedom can only
be discovered
through effort, diligence,
perseverance, devotion;
But that doesn't matter, awakening
awakening is what matters
awakening is that which matters, that which really takes no effort
that is what matters, that subtle effortless awakening;
Birth, dreams, death, rebirth, death birth death
returning, becoming any number of personages,
becoming lowly slime, becoming a god,
it doesn't matter at all, not in the least,
birth, death, birth, death becoming
becoming this or that,
an infinite array of beings from
uncountable worlds throughout the cosmos
in the void of deep space, through the quantum,
and beyond all known realities,
it is all controlled or losing control
controlled by what we cannot control,
losing control of this ignorant being,
or that ignorant luminosity,
this karmic control of all these actions,
control, control control?
Control that?
What is it that we are to control?
We cannot control that!
We cannot, not at all, not in the least, not even an iota of it,
we have no way whatsoever of controlling anything
unless we train the mind to consciously know what to do,
unless we train the mind in what is, as it is,

and, and and and this is no ordinary training, this is
persevering through rigorous conditions,
unthinkable adversities,
facing all those demons that want to rush in,
all those demons who are so familiar to you,
those demons you would rather never see again,
yet you see them again and again,
through all eternity,
hither and dabbling
in all the recurring lives, lifetimes
spent wasted without any inkling
about awakening
within this turbulent dream,
in all of this madness
from that which all seems oh-so impossible
to escape, to awaken;
With insight into what is going on here,
just what is going on here, now,
mastery
can be achieved,
so that the lives you follow, the lives you become,
the lives you live and die,
will not be random
random episodes of suffering and sorrow,
completely at their demise, your own demise,
of drifting through storms, uncontrollably,
life, death, birth, rebirth
repeating this nightmarish existence,
at the mercy of our
our own unknown actions,
at the mercy of that,
until we start
until we start to awaken,
we are at the mercy of that storm,
drifting in the ocean of uncertainty;
Begin to awaken, just start, just a little bit,
with a little effort leading to no effort,
with only that intention to awaken;
When compassion begins to swell
when we learn to see
as it is,
then our lives
your lives
will be
amazing

open-hearted
joy.

47

Karma,
these are just actions,
actions that are an illusion,
actions that spread to the far extremes
of this illusion, this ripple-effect
this action, those actions, that action
that little ineffectual
really bad thought changing your face to a scowl
that really destructive anger brewing in your gut
these destructive emotions create subtle changes
sometimes violent actions
sometimes just a twitch or a furled brow
a prune face emerging to cast doubt
a butterfly flapping its wings in disgust
a turtle hiding in a swamp;
all these actions emanate in all directions
outward inward sideways upways downways always;
beings are confused about this, this
this eternal echo emanating from actions;
This seems real enough, but then off it goes;
What becomes of that?
When will it come back?
These actions, those actions, lead to other actions,
amplifying, redirecting, coming back in unexpected ways;
It might be ten thousand lifetimes, or more,
before the fruition of that last angry gasp
comes back to you, that whatever-you-have-become by then,
and here you are just ignorantly not knowing, in lifetime after lifetime
not knowing
what is being carried
with your consciousness
not knowing a thing about that
not realizing
that you
matter,
that
you

matter,
that
your
actions
become
this
illusion.

48

What is this action
this unhappy action,
this eternal guilt
you have created,
this most repugnant act
you have done once more?
It is none other than that thing
preventing you from awakening
awakening to timeless luminosity;
It needs to go,
it needs a place to go,
or it will fester, eating away,
tearing you apart from that extraordinary light
apparently keeping you apart
from that which cannot be separate;
Disperse that nonsense!
Open yourself to the light
with great compassion
towards yourself, and all;
Give yourself a break!
You can't be serious about punishing
your self
through all eternity, just because
you do not know what you were doing;
Disperse that nonsense at once!
Enter the light for good!
Can you not see you were never something else?
Is it really unknown that you have always,
always been light,
that all-good eternal bright light?
What is this nonsense?
What is this nonsense where you think

you think you are apart from that?
Disperse that dread and guilt, at once!
Do this and it will mean nothing, it will be
dispersed into emptiness;
SPLOOSH!
It will be dispersed completely
if you give it nothing
nothing to do;
That pervasive confusion needs,
it needs an enchanting condition,
a sort of situation that beguiles us
into wanting more of that nightmare
a situation where we keep it going on forever;
It needs fruition of the condition, it needs
it needs something keeping our attention,
before it can become anything, before it becomes, becomes
something set forth from that action, that confused action
where you did not know what you were doing;
Not knowing is the cause of that
before it can occur to the senses, within this illusion,
it needs something else, something else;
Striking a match means
nothing, without oxygen,
lighting a candle
cannot be done
without
fire;
To extinguish
the causes and conditions
of our own mind's confusion
of our own actions instigated
by mind,
we must
remove attachment, let go!
Attachment to that most unfortunate fixation
that guilty dread, where we punish ourselves
we punish ourselves for all eternity
by preventing our own awakening,
seeking like-minded devotees
to closed minded punishment
what is the point to that?
Attachment beguiles us into
becoming that confused anxious being who suffers
who fixates on endlessly perpetuating
perpetuating more suffering,

that being who remains
in a state of confusion
creating more actions
that bring tears to our eyes,
giving us an excuse not to awaken
awaken to that most amazing light that is naturally present;
HO HO HO!
Just what do you think this will prove?
Just what do you think you are really doing?
You can't punish who you really are,
you can't give yourself
an eternal beating
that means
anything;
Your real nature, your primordial condition
is unlimited love and compassion,
see that,
know for sure that that is who you really are,
see that way you are keeping yourself
unaware;
Just look
at that situation,
that nonsensical cause,
we must look
at
that.

49

As I contemplate
this view
in this moment, I see
Dharmakaya,
that timeless luminosity, ever-present,
in this moment of clarity;
Now I see
three kayas carrying me,
this person I imagine myself to be,
through this moment,
upon imagined vehicles of mind;
I see this physical body;
I see energetic cognizant aspects;
I see that all-pervasive bright wisdom, intensity beyond thought,

beyond imagination, beyond any reification,
beyond our shared struggle,
but not out there, in here, in this cognizant moment of mind;
This is not so difficult, as people seem to think;
This moment can be seen in its entirety
by just resting in that state of being, then seeing clearly,
inwardly, what is oh-so-obvious,
as it is,
not trying to believe something,
not trying to fabricate some meaning
not trying to apply dreamt-up structure, to this
hallucination;
We don't need a notion to carry us trembling
trembling through cold turbulent seas of delusion
heavy under clouds, masked by fog,
with winds biting us, tearing our skin away,
where we are brutally, viciously, oblivious,
about our real condition, that which cannot be escaped;
We don't need imagined bright horizons
in our mind, carrying us to imagined places, beyond the clouds,
beyond obscurations, a destination for us to go;
That clear space is right here,
at all times, in this moment;
It is utterly screaming at us to notice;
It is for us to see freely, clearly, without any hesitation,
with ease, without moving
without moving at all;
All that magnificent splendor of our real nature,
all, all we need for complete freedom, is
is simply here,
not before us, not out there,
it is within us,
as it is, in this
eternal moment of
great
compassion.

50

Holding onto life,
we see danger everywhere;
Our ego clings to this life

not knowing what awaits,
fearful of death and our demise;
Embracing death, our life becomes fulfilled
through peaceful contemplation
becoming at ease with this
this inevitable transference
this inevitable gap between
between this life and the next;
Without preparation, our next life
will become, once again, one of confusion
ignorance and turmoil;
Listening
to our own
inner voice, our intuition,
we find peace,
we find satisfaction
that it is as it is,
as we prepare for death;
Deep contemplation into this
state of being,
this life, this perplexity,
this ongoing nervousness,
this dangerous, joyful,
sadness-ridden,
spiteful, hateful, fear-filled, ignorant,
obnoxious, what-havya-macallits,
thing we call life
this life really never
never ever seems to bring
anything whatsoever that lasts,
not a single lasting note,
not of any kind,
it's all just sort of, remarkably like
some horrible nonsense,
stuff you can't get out of
no matter what,
this life,
this
life,
this, this, life
this life that doesn't ever go away,
even upon death,
as we become aware of cyclic existence,
that illusion of death being only a gap,
a gap that keeps happening, our life just keeps

keeps us confused and fretful, keeps
happening, happening happening
pulling us back to more of that,
that turmoil that binds us
with ignorance, aversion, desire,
over and over again, this cycle spinning
spins out of control, enchanting us into more of that,
that fixation that grasping at life itself,
this life ends, then we walk
we walk through another door, into
into another life, another set of circumstances,
where we find that last thought in that previous life
that next thought in this life
leading to that last thought in this life
becomes, becomes
that first thought in the next life, this life,
and again, in the next, and the next and onward,
onward upward downward
through all eternity, it doesn't matter,
it's the same mad way, it is all the same exact way
again and again, and yet we go on and on
thinking this moment is all,
thinking we are the same person that we were
from one moment to the next, in this life,
the next lives, all lives,
like mirrors reflecting onto themselves
for all eternity, in all directions,
and here we are in this madness,
thinking we are separate,
or that consciousness itself goes on
in utter madness;
How is that, that within
this insanity, this condition of disquiet
ever really anything?
How can it be
this or that?
How can we, you,
how can we ever be
worried
about anything?
I mean really, we're never ever
never actually, we can't be real,
we can't be destroyed,
this figment of our own doing,
we're just temporary,

an illusion, created by our own
vivid
imagination.

51

Trying desperately
to see
that which is beyond thought
is complete futility,
it becomes obvious at some point, at some point
as we practice inner reflection,
we learn through that, that way
through direct experience, upon
catching glimpses of our real nature,
it becomes obvious
at some point
it becomes apparent that effort cannot
effort cannot show us that;
When it is this pervasive, this subtle condition,
we cannot merely bludgeon it with that great mallet
of our mind, through effort,
bombarding it with thoughts, beliefs,
notions that escape us completely, we cannot
expect nonsense clutter noise confusion
to help us in the least, it is folly to think so,
the problem of being attached to that, that is
that is the issue, we delude ourselves
expecting results of any kind;
we remain confused when, when,
we apply those things that
bind us to our insanity,
that perpetuate the crazy,
the crazy in us that keeps us confused;
When we are at ease, oh so relaxed
when we are completely at rest
aware in that
moment,
in that
condition,
only then
can we see clearly,
can we glimpse

glimpse what we have known
since beginningless time,
that which is beyond
intellect,
that which is
always
just there
in our
every
forever moment.

52

That place you have never left, that bright place
timeless luminosity, that clear space beyond reason
that intense brightness we become upon death,
that amazing brilliance we forget with life,
that condition beyond self, beyond fabrication, beyond thought,
our real primordial condition from timeless beginninglessness
bright beyond all ordinary intensity, that real nature of our mind,
held so dear, held so tightly that it cannot be found
it is so subtle, so obvious, that we miss it altogether;
What makes you think you have somewhere to go?
Why should we pretend to look elsewhere
in this spiritual journey of returning
returning to where we have always been?
Why should we find any sort of comfort
in all those childish beliefs, created by mind?
One must not conflate, one must not confuse
the nature of mind with mind,
or anything that mind creates,
as mind in motion creates all this confusion;
One must also not think, not think,
that mind and the nature of mind
are two, they're not, they're not two!
Don't forget that!
All this fabrication of beliefs,
all those foolish ideations, that confuse us,
that is why we find ourselves
we find ourselves poisoned by our own
state of mind creating actions;
Nature of mind, emanating
emanating continuously without moving,

as timeless luminosity here,
here where we are, reflecting that
that amazing wisdom brightness,
into our every perfect moment,
perfect from the beginning,
Dharmakaya;
One is not other from that,
and, yet, that is not the same
as when we are fixed upon magical illusions
in our gaze that cannot be without dazzling wisdom
in every moment of our lives, though confused,
without awareness, that cannot be separate;
Though only our confusion makes that so;
There it is in all of that magnificence, that
that brightness beyond all brightness;
How can we not know?
How can we not know that we have not left that,
any of that, behind?
We have not gone anywhere,
we have not become something else,
we have not become something,
we are not anything that we can point to,
we are just an infinitely occurring reflection,
emanating with infinite possibilities,
emanating throughout this mad dream,
this insanity of our own creation;
Though it is so fantastic, so magical,
so amazing to imagine, to fabricate, to create
this self, this fictitious being that we invent,
the pain is also truly horrendous,
this being, this person,
appearing out of light,
identical, simply identical
to that reflection in the mirror,
confusion dictates that one is not aware
not aware of the reflection and appearance;
It only becomes real, this being that appears,
when we become that integrated presence,
mind getting into the nature of mind, the same as that,
through deep contemplative practice, or death,
shedding our unawareness, mind
going into that reflection of its own nature
with infinite possibilities, unlimited potentiality,
letting this silly notion,
this fantasy self,

completely dissolve, into that brilliant bright light,
to utterly disappear into that
brilliance beyond reason, simply appearing there,
aware of this condition as it is, not as we wish it to be;
Just as the mirror itself reflects only
what is placed in front of that,
only what mind cooks up from an infinite recipe book,
the nature of mind is simply
as it is, not this fabricated ego,
simply as it is, without reification,
beyond artificial ideas;
It is better to take
ultimate refuge in the three kayas, rather
rather than continuing in confusion;
Take refuge in the ultimate state of timeless luminosity,
take refuge in the energetic cognizant state,
take refuge in the emanation body
that appears to mind in this world,
knowing that it is inseparable
and not different
from that bright light
beyond all bright lights,
brighter than a billion stars,
that pervasive expansive
ultimate condition,
and yet, it
it appears simply as
as a creation of mind,
not
real.

53

Happiness
happiness is really just the only thing we want, happiness
when we wander, we want happiness
that first key, when we take our first step
on that amazing spiritual journey,
reuniting our amazing life with that luminous presence
that timeless luminosity beyond all reason;
Happiness is that key which opens us to kindness,
so, it is not to be dismissed as unimportant,

and kindness is that key that opens us to happiness;
Kindness
such a simple key to discover, such an easy path to take
nothing could be more simple than this notion of being kind
and look at that!
That key, kindness, that very easy key to acquire,
that key where we decide to be kind to ourselves and others,
not offending anyone, if you can help it
deciding to live a life of virtue, not harming,
being generous, offering a kind word,
that easy key is the key to compassion;
Compassion,
when we see ourselves in others,
when we see that we are all connected,
when our heart breaks when we see
death, sickness, old age, pain and suffering
when we see this futility in life,
when, when this life and death cycle
when it becomes apparent
because it reveals inwardly to us how others feel
because it instills within us a yearning to help others
we discover the key of compassion, we can't help it,
the yearning to help others overwhelms,
so, compassion arises, naturally, without being fully aware
that compassion is the key to great compassion;
Great Compassion,
which flows to all, from all, encompassing all beings
with this desire to alleviate all suffering,
all of this pain in the world, pain, we must understand the root
the root of that pain and suffering,
so, we see that there is nothing
nothing we can do to help, nothing whatsoever,
we see our efforts all leading to futile actions,
but our compassion is so great, this key
this key is so important, as we grow to know that
unless we see that all beings must awaken,
if beings do not awaken, there will be no relief from suffering
in this endless cycle of birth, living, dying and dreams,
falling apart through sickness or old age, death and birth again
in each moment, all that stuff of our turbulent existence,
leading to that understanding that
great compassion is so important,
such an important key, that it must be
it must be used at once, for its purpose
its purpose is too great to hold tight,

great compassion is the key to Bodhicitta;
Aspiring for Bodhicitta,
that notion that we wish to be on the path of awakening
so that all beings will awaken, through our great compassion,
and, if we aspire long enough, we discover the key,
the key to ending suffering for others,
which is so precious, such an amazing find;
Relative Bodhicitta,
which is this understanding that we must first awaken,
we must first awaken or help others to awaken,
so, we diligently go down that path, seeking our own
enlightenment,
and that of others,
helping everyone or being ready to help all,
helping them to awaken before we
before we awaken entirely,
and if we do this long enough,
we discover an ultimate key
the key to everything, which liberates itself
which is the key called
Absolute Bodhicitta,
which really has no name, being beyond such things
being beyond ordinary thought
understanding of our real nature;
Bodhicitta,
on the absolute level,
is the key to everything,
it is freedom,
it is liberation from that which binds us,
it dispels all karma,
it is the ultimate,
it is that which radiates from timeless luminosity,
Dharmakaya essence,
it is
when
we
Awaken.

54

When we've seen that great bright expanse,
that brightness beyond all brilliant intensity,
when we've come to know that
through death or trauma or mystical experience
remembering
we remember what it is that we have witnessed
or experienced in our heart, in our mind,
directly experiencing that perfect state,
that state we recognize when we awaken,
when we yearn to return, to that,
we yearn to be exactly that,
whatever that is, beyond perfection,
we yearn for that when we remember
beyond ideas, beyond thoughts of divinity or beyond,
beyond any sort of notion that we might have,
while under this guise, this ignorant state of affairs,
that which binds us to this cycle
this eternal cycle of our own suffering,
this life-death-life and death again cycle
in this moment of delusion
this delusion where we think
we think all things are permanent
where we drift aimlessly, aimlessly
through immense pain and sadness,
constantly buffeted by waves
waves of our own painful life,
dreams where we yearn,
we yearn for death,
we yearn so deeply
for that death-state,
between old age and birth,
we have but a moment, which seems eternal,
a moment of comfort, just a moment
of eternal wisdom bringing us comfort,
and we see with clarity what we must do,
we see through ultimate compassion that we must awaken,
we must awaken at our very next opportunity;
But, instead, we forget, again and again we flounder
we forget our primary wisdom knowledge,
focusing on the delusionary object of our life

that we create for ourselves, as we have always done,
thinking that we have become some god or something real,
for an instant, we think that
reifying that condition, as we grasp at desire,
feeling exhilarated, so we cling with desire to life,
rather than seeing that direct experience,
seeing that for what it is,
beyond all thought, beyond ideas, beyond this life
beyond this physical existence of endless pain and suffering
beyond this stream of reified reality,
we, instead, see only our ignorant condition,
calling it self or me, or some other name,
reifying that,
thinking it
is real;
What we have told ourselves
repeatedly, repeatedly
throughout this consciousness stream
throughout beginningless eons
across untold dimensions
in all the world systems
in all the infinite universes,
in each and every clear moment
we tell ourselves to awaken,
we have told ourselves every time
before we return to a physical body
that we must, by all means available,
develop that intention to awaken, we,
then we must begin this awakening
then when we must awaken when
when we have the opportunity
when we have the ability
when for sure, we must,
or there is no hope
of remaining
as bright
wisdom
light.

55

Awakening
in this moment
is not beyond the possibilities
of mind, it is
it is what you have always been
before this
before this magical delusional
before this egotistical
maniacal
psychotic
fixation
took root in your being
in this thing you have confused
for being somebody,
for being something other,
for living
a life,
before you went down that rabbit hole
of crazed delusion,
thinking you were
separate.
Crazy.
Imbecilic.
Insane.
Just wake up
crazy mixed-up being!
Awaken right now
and you
will
see.

56

Awakening
becoming fully aware all at once,
just once
once more aware of that great light
that intense light we have seen repeatedly every time
every time we die

that great inexplicable brilliantly intense infinite light
that light that we become, that is never separate
that light of this amazing explosive eternal moment, just now
awakening into our real primordial condition
awakening into this easiest thing that we can ever do,
awakening into what is automatic, natural, subtle . . . obvious
like walking without moving, through a doorway into bright light
like bright light enveloping our every moment of being,
awakening takes no effort whatsoever, it is so subtle that effort obstructs,
awakening is really only possible without the slightest effort,
though it does not seem possible;

Let go! Let go! Let go!

Timeless luminosity awaits in every moment!
Primordial awakening awaits here and now!
Awakening requires more than just intention, much much more than that
our guru of that most infinite light, our real nature of mind,
our guru must help us to ignite that most intense bright wisdom of
awakening
that most extreme intention for awakening, great compassion to awaken
great compassion for our own lives becoming present in awareness
compassion for diligent effort, that effort which has been our habit
our habit from timeless beginnings, that habit of effort and clinging
skillfully applied, breaking all bad habits clinging to us from
timeless beginnings,
so, we must apply effort, and persevere and be diligent about it
so that we can have no effort;

HO HO HO!

That cosmic joke of our own unawareness must become our path;
Awakening only happens with impossibly diligent
perseverance, devotion to practice,
obtaining strength, confronting impossible demons
transforming, self-liberating, fearlessly
confronting demons that have stopped us until now,
those demons that are waiting to attack some more,
from time immemorial, demons that have been tormenting us,
we need to prepare, prepare to meet them
meet them with no effort whatsoever;
Ignorance and delusion, desire and repulsion,
keystones of our very bad habit of thinking we are real,
these poisons of our lives take unbelievable amounts
unbelievable amounts of effort, of commitment to being tattered,

commitment to being shredded alive in this crazy swirling
dream-like state of being;
To generate karma that can help, actions, we must
we must keep in mind that ultimate guru, the one we all know so well,
beyond time and space, and any sort of thought
that timeless nature of mind guru, the guru who can help us
help us to become awakened, helping us to see that
we must fabricate ideas in order to overcome
ideas, fabricating
fabricating ideas that help, fabricating ideas that teach us,
in order to let go of ideas about this and that,
even letting go of ideas about awakening, we must
apply that sort of effort, until there is no
effort;
We cry to the heavens that we are in terrible
terrible anguish, we need help,
yet here we are with nothing available
nothing to do available right here now,
which is the most helpful thing ever;
Through our anguish,
we must see that amazing
contradiction, that infinite joke of being
where we can understand
that all is good;
Rest in that natural state, confused beings, rest
as it is;
Oh, wandering beings, rest
without changing anything,
without continuing with this great effort
of personhood,
just
awaken,
awaken
just
like
that!

SNAP!

57

Sometimes
on rare occasion
we wander into the human realm,
where it is most fortunate, and conducive for awakening;
Sometimes we wander into the animal realm,
where we are in constant fear of everything,
because of our stupidity;
Sometimes we wander into hell,
due to anger burning us,
and, with such suffering we yearn for escape,
we wish we had some sort of chance;
Sometimes we are in a place of mind where there are
hungry ghosts, ever-greedy, with no possibility of satisfaction;
Sometimes we wander into the state of asuras,
ever at war with the gods, very jealous;
Sometimes we wander into the god realm,
and though we are filled with great pleasure,
having every opportunity imaginable,
we squander this, not ever wanting to see it end,
and in the end of this
we experience terrible anger,
plunging us at once into that state of mind of hell;
These are just states of mind
which appear to us
in different
conditions of manifestation,
these are just the places we wander
while in this deluded condition
of our lives
illusion unending;
Without understanding our
states of mind,
we cannot hope
to escape
further
suffering,
and so we wander.

58

Within that infinite dream, that very very long dream, we dream
we dream so many many small dreams,
and within that, those, those many many more small dreams
we forget what we have forgotten in each moment
we have so many many uncountable thoughts
passing us by without us taking notes
just in this day or through years, or
through eons without beginning,
within this eternal now,
thoughts seem so unending
in this active busy motion of mind
ripples, splashing, exploding
thoughts that ignite our imaginations
thinking, always thinking, that this is real, or that
thinking that this that is real,
thinking, oh, now we have the answer, forgetting,
thinking, no, then we had the answer, or that before
that which we witnessed before that, that was it!
We think we know that answer that
thinking everything we see is real,
we keep thinking that,
and then we discover that all that stuff,
that stuff is not real, none of it is real
this dream within a dream within a dream
it is just our life appearing,
it is not real;
This stuff we discover in our daily life
is just the stuff of dreams within dreams,
within this illusion of time
it's a very long dream, where
we live and die and live again, and dream
though we can also sleep within that dream,
for anything is possible in this infinite array of possibilities
within that life, or through other dreams
where we have even longer dreams within that;
All that experience of death within dreams,
death as well, death
seems real enough, just like those dreams
though it is simply our natural condition
passing us by, reflections through a prism,
as we transmigrate, as we return once more

into this cycle of dreams within dreams,
completely losing what illusion we thought we were,
death, then life, then that gap of death again,
it is just that space between dreams,
that illusion between illusions, another
illusion of mind;
Though more real than reality itself,
it is not
real.

59

Examine this stuff, this stuff
stuff that you think is solid, look at it
closely,
LOOK!
Look at that solid appearance you think is there,
look at how it really is, just look
look at how it is changing
aging, falling apart over time, in this moment
look at the molecules and atoms,
look deeper still, look
look into the core of quantum
experience,
look at life and death and all that other stuff
look, look at it that way or this way,
it doesn't matter, just look
it was one thing, and then it is another,
never the same for more than one instant,
never real for even a moment,
just look, look
deeper and deeper
into that, just look
into the fabric of time and space,
look into the appearance
of the universe
all that stuff in your mind,
look at all the rising and falling of stars
throughout infinite eons, throughout
expansions and contractions
of multiple universes
from beginningless time;

How can this solid stuff be real?
This stuff, what is that?
What is that notion
of solidity?
What is this
thought?
How arrogant
it is
of you to think
any of it
is
real.

60

Don't get me wrong,
this appearance is not real, and
neither is death,
however, that experience of death,
when the bright light comes, merging
merging with what you thought you once were,
where you completely lose and forget who you were
when the intensity of a billion suns shine upon you in that moment
when it becomes brightness beyond madness, with a trillion universes
merged into that single moment that lasts an eternity
when you are indistinguishable from eternal timeless luminosity
inseparable from primordial wisdom
in that moment of death,
it will be more real than anything you have ever experienced
it will be more real than each and every moment of your life,
it will be more real than anything your imagination can tell you;
and, yet,
that experience
is also just an illusion,
just something beyond
our imaginations,
beyond reason,
it cannot be
reified
not in the least,
death
is beyond
any

notion
of being,
that way is
simply
as
it
is.

61

Pure vision
is always here,
present though we just can't see, the obvious
the obvious that is completely hidden, hidden from us,
we cannot see that we always have pure vision
always, at all times, radiance of primordial wisdom,
we can't see because we are distracted by this or that,
we can't see because of our supreme effort not to see,
focusing on not having pure vision, this or that,
obsessing about staying away
hiding ourselves from sanity;
With our deluded ways,
that take so much
effort,
we do everything we can
to remain deceived by unreality,
to remain un-realized,
asleep, confused, deluded,
ignorant,
lost in pain and suffering;
We choose
to reject
pushing away that pure vision
which has been lovingly given to us,
which we give freely to ourselves,
which has always been just there,
which is naturally present
in every moment,
we decide that
we must
feed
feed our bad habit
our bad habit of grasping and fixation,

we choose insanity over sanity,
we do this through effort,
because of
pure vision,
through our
natural
state
of being;

OM
AH
HUM!
HUM!
HUM!

62

People will seek the most profound teachings,
looking for the cream of the very best that is profound,
and once they have found that, will egotistically proclaim
they will proclaim that they are now enlightened
having found the answer to it all, despite
despite not really knowing what those teachings mean;
It is better, by far, to seek the lowest teachings,
to honestly build the foundation first, to not be in a hurry,
just relax, take it step by step, clear up all those misunderstandings
that are held by mind through ignorance and ego,
practice obliterating all those obstacles to knowing the true nature of mind,
practice opening your heart and mind to possibilities beyond thought
practice seeing everything as it is
practice seeing what is beyond, beyond life and death
practice listening to breath with concentrative equipoise
practice looking into mind
practice observing thoughts, as they arise
and doing nothing whatsoever with them
practice remaining mindful within this energetic condition
practice learning;
If we can practice all of that, then
we can
begin
perfecting
at some point,
when we are ready

ready to reveal to ourselves
that most profound ordinariness;
and so
it is our
task
to become
ready
for
awakening.

63

Being trapped in this cycle of our own creation, we look
we look for a way to escape, from that,
we look, we seek, we search
for answers to this most perplexing problem
of being, of just what is appearing,
we seek, we look at all that happening
right before our eyes,
appearances dancing before us,
lulling us into a deep sleep,
without knowing we are asleep,
keeping us from knowing;
We have trapped ourselves this way!
We have hidden
what it is
that we already
know;
We have become so
immersed in sleep
that we forget
that
that which has shown itself repeatedly
time and time again,
just in the last moment, really
just in every moment, we forget that
that infinite knowledge,
we become
unable
unable to shake this confusion
our mind fixates, freezes,
we lose our way forward,
not that there ever has been

a way forward, something out there,
something that we can point to;
That dream logic
that way of knowing when we are completely open,
that makes no sense whatsoever in daily life,
that makes no sense when we are formulating beliefs
or concocting that confused way we think of things,
thinking we are somehow separate,
it is really that same openness
it is that same clarity
that clarity of death,
death clarity, all else is just
something we create,
some sort of structure
for our thoughts
within this very
long dream
of life.

64

Some say
that confusion is
just the clouds
out there up in the sky, far away,
external obstacles which keep us
from seeing that bright light
that light that is always there present beyond
out there someplace, out there, somewhere
out there in the distance;
No! I say to you, that a profound error!
That is not it at all!
Timeless luminosity is always present!
That bright eternal light, beyond reason
is within, outside and beyond, all at once!
Confusion, that most precious commodity
that condition you protect more than any other
is that state of not knowing
which keeps you
from seeing that bright
brilliant
timeless wisdom
emanating from clear luminosity

right here within, right in this moment, now
without doing anything, without having to remove clouds;
This primordial wisdom remains
in each moment;
Your clouds are just your own fabrication,
something you have created, no different than confusion itself,
there can be nothing to see out there, don't focus on that!
If you cannot see this bright light
If you cannot see within yourself, then don't look at that
object beyond, that simile, that example, that parable that, that
that representation is not the experience,
clouds of mind are nothing to be concerned with,
take no special notice, whatever you do!
Don't look out there, beyond that!
Look here now!
Look inwardly at mind;
When you see that your own mind
has created those clouds
out there,
then you
can
begin to see
true wisdom;
It's
only
as it is.

65

Just this, just that
we believe all sorts of useless things,
grasping at anything, at nothing,
inventing this and that,
creating all that we see,
creating all these useless beliefs,
for no apparent reason,
other than fear,
other than not knowing, not knowing
what it is that our senses show us,
or delight of what is not real,
all that mind perceives
in this confused state,
we grasp without knowing,

we grasp, then defend that grasping,
thinking we must know anything,
thinking we have found the answer
in this or that useless belief,
without knowing that all beliefs are completely
without value, completely useless;
When we
examine what it is that we think,
we discover through that inquiry that
all thoughts fall apart, all
concepts dissolve upon looking;
Just as it is, that is all
all we need to know, it is as it is,
we only need to know that
that all that is
empty cognizance
originating from clarity
clarity of the nature of mind,
that very same timeless luminosity
that bright light of eternity,
that which we encounter
when we have died;
All that appears is
not from substantial
existence,
not from
solid form,
not
from isness,
not from beingness, not
from anything the universe has to offer,
not a product of belief, nothing
nothing that can be described
as
substantial.

66

Without intention
we cannot awaken,
we cannot awaken into to that timeless luminosity
we cannot become aware, aware of that intense bright light,
though every opportunity presents itself, intention,

intention is required if we wish to awaken to what is
just there, that timeless state we have met in death
over and over again as we transmigrate across circumstance;
Though teachings rain down on us from the heavens,
though great enlightened masters come to us with all we need,
and gods appear before us with treasures of the heart,
though we discover texts with all answers in them
answers to all of the most profound questions,
without our very sincere honest
intention
intention to awaken,
nothing will happen,
we will only
go on
as before
riding this wave of life and death
swirling around in this turbulence of being
getting old or pummeled by illness;
Suffering, being
oblivious to our true condition in this world,
going from one place of misery to another
one ever-changing place of agony or nervousness,
or despair,
we stay that way, angsting
in general,
even if
we have a moment
or two
of peace,
of relief
happiness or bliss;
Without true intention to
awaken, to go beyond,
without that,
expect
nothing
other than yearning for that bright light,
expect what has always been,
pain
unending.

67

Though it is not
obvious
to us, though
we are not aware
of that state of our being,
we are in that state at all times,
though we think we cannot escape,
thinking this is how we have been
for all eternity, before many beginnings,
this is what we are for all eternity, unless we escape
where we have found ourselves repeating uncounted lifetimes
in this condition where we see ourselves dying
repeatedly, again and again, death presents itself to us,
we take that hysterical ride
from one lifetime to another,
we cringe when we know our body has failed us,
we can only be confused by that, wandering in unsatisfactoriness,
facing all our demons and the winds that howl across time,
thinking this or that, unaware of our awareness,
unaware of our own unawareness,
making up stories, inventing beliefs, having ideas,
seeking comfort in that sense,
that feeling of dis-ease,
seeking answers about that inexplicable
that amazing reality surrounding our lives,
surrounding our death journey,
that is just there in life, here in this moment,
not far away, not hard to encounter,
timeless luminosity
not in any way beyond this condition where we are now;
It's ironical, wouldn't you say?
Here we are searching for a way to awaken, and we have no idea,
we have no idea about what is going on, about that
that, that, condition where we find ourselves, we
have no idea about that, we fret instead, ignoring
that luminous condition;
It's really very amusing, really, really isn't it?
We have only to awaken from this dream
but here we are feeling helpless
feeling trapped, though we have everything, we
we all have everything we need for ultimate freedom;

HA HA HA, HO!
This blazing light of our
true primordial
condition,
this ultimate
awareness
is just
right
here
now.

68

Although we may hear this or that,
sometimes thinking that
that we are already enlightened,
or living perfectly,
or something like that,
that we shouldn't walk down a path,
thinking that we are gods,
or some other amazing type of being,
maybe we think we are already awake,
or that nobody is here to be awake,
thinking, thinking, always thinking egotistically
thinking it is time to be as reckless as we can be, thinking
we could do nothing, it won't matter, so just forget about it,
or just go back into ignorance, cultivate delusion or bad feelings,
thinking we were wrong to seek, or to ask questions;
Wise masters will say
you should avoid that, those traps,
they will say don't destroy what is precious, don't fall into traps,
we think without knowing, without being certain, we blunder, we form
we formulate very wrong ideas about this or that,
confidently blundering our way through life,
not realizing that we must show great compassion for all,
instead, here we are busily, so very busily
twisting and contorting the truth of the matter,
misunderstanding the essence of how we
how we should spend our time opening
opening our heart and mind, instead
here we are arbitrarily recklessly indulgently
leading ourselves astray with total confidence
in that, in that nonsense we have discovered,

without knowing the full extent
of what it is we should know,
foolishly paying no heed to wisdom holders or gurus,
or the warnings they have expressed,
we wander off to our old ways of deceiving
deceiving ourselves, in the same ways we have always done,
after all we have discovered, we throw it away
we discard this most precious gem as if it were garbage,
here we are growing closed and hard crusted
when we are at the brink of luminous existence, we deceive
deceiving ourselves at the worst possible moment,
we must understand what we do,
venturing into folly that way,
losing our compassion
compassion that is essential to ourselves and others;

Pay heed! This illusion is poisoned!

It is poisoned by ignorance, attraction and aversion,
this poison that has overtaken us
in this condition, as it always has been, throughout many lifetimes
in this state of continual cyclic suffering,
it is a chain that we must break
in order to become aware,
aware of what has eluded us and deluded us,
our cognizance of that tends to be lacking,
lacking in urgency,
lacking in compassion;
We must practice to go beyond,
to free ourselves, by looking
by looking at mind, honestly seeing
seeing to overcome, opening
opening our heart and mind so that we may overcome
overcome that which binds us, looking in order to do nothing
where nothing is necessary,
looking in order to do something, when we must;
These ideas about what to do, what not to do,
gradual or sudden expansive wisdom, grab us, hook us,
commit ourselves to many wrong ideas,
leading us astray by our own thoughts
our own thoughts, which are not honest;
How can this be?
Ignorance is part of mind's play,
not really existing,
not really not existing,

not really anything we can point to
or discover upon gazing
gazing into mind or imagination or phenomena,
and yet, these thoughts are not real,
it is simply a magical illusion, a reflection when
when we see it with thought, when we think it is real,
and yet, to those who are deceived,
ignorance is powerful!
We must persevere in our endeavor,
endeavor to develop great compassion
for ourselves in our precious endeavor of becoming
becoming permanently ultimately compassionately aware
becoming open and aware through our compassion;
This great compassion is the key that opens
radiantly opens our hearts and mind
to our real ultimate condition,
timeless luminosity
in this illusion unfolding,
this subtle dream,
this cyclic existence,
which continues
indefinitely
now.

69

For those who die
who die and then come back
to life in the same body, as
before, infinite blessings abound, for
those beings have tasted primordial wisdom
recalling what has eluded them in life,
remembering it as just so amazing;
This leads to a yearning that is so deep, yearning
to return to that, that which seems so much like home, that
that infinite expanse, that luminous glow, that
that wisdom beyond all reason, that that
that timeless state of blessing beyond being
beyond all that can reasonably be ascertained;
That yearning is yearning, just yearning
for something that is never
apart

from this moment, this life,
that taste of a pure expansive bright light is not
beyond
what is here now;
To remain living, while knowing that,
to remain in that knowledge is a blessing beyond all blessings,
there is no returning, we cannot return, because
you
have
never
left
that;
To know this while living, one must train the mind,
or reflect upon the last time you were dead,
one must look introspectively, at that,
one must relax, resting in that natural state of being,
one must endeavor to awaken to that, now,
awakening to what we already know, though we have forgotten,
one
must
merely
see that;
So, sit in this moment, without distraction, training in that,
to not be distracted in the least,
do that for one moment, then do that for the next
moment, and the next
moment,
in time
this life
appears as
that
infinite
brightness,
timeless luminosity.

70

Seeing in death
seeing that we have manifested
thus manifested
in life,
seeing that this energy manifestation
of being

has arisen out of emptiness and cognizance
beyond beyond,
beyond our every waking moment
we see that it becomes one of yearning
yearning for that state of pure clarity
bright expansive timeless, extremely brilliant clarity
in that state beyond death
where we have seen our true nature, our true guru,
within the gap that is regarded
as death, that infinite expanse
we yearn, upon returning,
for that most excellent
state of being,
we yearn for that,
though we know in our heart
that we have never left
that;
With this deep yearning
we find a heavy need
to always be aware
of that,
and, so, we
must
persevere;
We must find another who has seen that, who can help us
to see our true guru, who was there for us
to see beyond beyond, beyond
that which restricts our knowing,
beyond that which limits us
in any way, beyond
beyond thought;
And, in this way,
we must persevere
to practice
the ultimate practice
the practice of seeing the inexplicable,
being aware of that light
that light which cannot be described
that amazing bright light
at all times
seeing
our
true
guru.

71

Becoming timeless
ultimate light, explosive brightness,
when this happens, no language can explain,
nothing can be conceived at all
nothing can help you understand what that is,
that condition goes well beyond the bounds we understand,
going far beyond knowing, beyond ideas of knowing,
in this natural state of no limitations, that is so familiar, life arises,
life, that dull condition of not knowing, not being
particularly aware of this or that in that dull place
of confusion,
being anxiously confused, unsettled
in a world of physical beauty,
that place where we forget,
magically forgetting,
where we do the impossible
by forgetting
through dream logic, and also
forgetting dream reasoning itself,
forgetting notions of our real nature;
It is simply that we are not resting in that
primordial state of being
that state we have known all along, that we are all familiar with
over eons of very interesting encounters of being in that death bardo,
that gap between lives, where we merely forget what seems real
in each lifetime, as problems arise, as our wisdom gets muddy;
Time, thought, ideas of a physical reality, language,
all become not very important, truly ridiculous
when we are in that timeless luminosity
that primordial state of being that is our real condition;
This idea of self and other becomes ridiculous,
because there is really no difference
when we are in that aware state;
If you were still attached to this ridiculous idea of self,
as it is in lifetime after lifetime,
as it is in an out-of-body experience,
then, of course,
you would still retain language, memories,
problems, because only of that attachment to life;
Beyond that, all words all
language would be forgotten,

at least temporarily
in that space between either going forward or going back,
all problems are forgotten, life's concerns,
attachments to this and that, grasping, grasping goes away,
everything dissolves into that moment of pure wisdom
wisdom timelessly, for an eternity
of knowing in the ultimate sense,
just
like
that.

72

Without the Guru of the Body,
Nirmanakaya,
we cannot begin to walk on the Path,
our physical manifestation would remain
encumbered by all that ails us;
Without the Guru of Voice, of Energetic Cognizance,
Sambhogakaya,
we cannot hope to Transform,
as the teachings would have no effect on us;
Without the Guru of Mind, Emptiness,
Dharmakaya,
we will not recognize our real nature;
Without all three elements,
without this most perfect Trinity
of body, energetic voice and mind
we cannot possibly attain Realization;

OM AH HUNG!

These are your Gurus,
to think otherwise
is to not know
the Guru;
This Trinity,
this indestructible Vajra,
is your real true
Guru;
Such is the manifestation
of all,
of all that is suchness, of all that is complete,

free from any sort of conceptual elaboration,
beyond all that we know;
To be devoted to that
is
real
devotion,
unencumbered by
confusion,
doubt
or
poison.

73

When you see that, that
that timeless luminosity beyond all that can be conceived, that
amazing nature of mind
when you recognize that real condition
that primordial consciousness of all-being, of all beyond,
all-pervasiveness in this present moment,
brightness beyond imagination,
brilliance beyond
reason,
when you see
that indescribableness beyond, beyond that
that which we cannot see with eyes, that
that which defies the formulation
of imagined imagery, ultimate,
being absolute in every way,
that, that that that which we can not say is that,
we can only point towards that, without being able
to describe, even to ourselves
we cannot reify or objectify
or justify that condition beyond
that infallible illusive state,
that all-pervasive
condition
that;
When we see that,
we are looking
at our own
true
guru.

74

Just look at that
when we die, just like that,
the ultimate guru, beyond all
arising in that incredible brightness, outside of time,
that which we were, we become once more,
that which we have always been
appears to us as we dissolve
into infinite wisdom;
Oh, it is so
magnificent to be home
in that primordial
state of being,
compassion,
love,
but, then,
the joke is on us;
We have never left!
Why did we think otherwise?

HO HO HO!!!

Just look
at all that
all that worry
we, one and all, have
have put ourselves through!
Look at that,
amazing
magical,
that, that
ultimate
guru
is
us.

75

I suppose
upon coming back into a physical body,
whether by rebirth or by not dying after all,
I suppose there is that clear moment, just as consciousness arises,
where we see the infinite timeless expanse
of our real nature, of that intense luminosity of Dharmakaya,
and we notice that our energetic state of consciousness
and colors and sound and rays of light,
swirling in that vibrational space
so small by comparison, so very small
we see little quivering bubbles
twirling about, some of which appear
as expansive heavens, so very small
and also, so very huge, for those with limited viewpoints,
and all of these swirling these-things and those-thats,
this is when we notice a very small dot
amid that, amid that
amazing Sambhogakaya,
this speck of physical being,
so very microscopic,
and even smaller than that,
much smaller than we can imagine small to be
we see that this dot within a dot is our immense universe,
we see that it is just one among an infinite array
of universes in a field of unending universes,
and we realize that this very small thing
which had seemed so large
once upon a time when we didn't know
when we were so small and confused
among it all, dependent
upon limited senses
and we
we then come back
into our
physical body,
Nirmanakaya;
In that state
we see
that we have known
three ultimate gurus
through

all of that
amazing
expanse
of
now.

76

Awareness
unborn, not created in the least bit,
naturally arises in each
spontaneous
moment,
very subtle;
Do you see that?
Or has your vision become so clouded that
that you do not even see glimpses of this happening?
Sit!
Breathe!
Pay Attention!
You are so distracted and fixated on what is not real
so distracted that you
that you do not see what is happening all around
in every luminous moment,
you!
This unborn state of being
is the essence
of consciousness;
It cannot be located
nor found
nor identified
nor reified in any manner,
nor can it be conceptualized
nor discovered through ideas
and intellect;
It is right here!
It is there!
It is everywhere!
It is beyond everywhere!
What is your problem?
Just get in that awareness
right NOW!

77

In all directions, in all times,
continuity of our real condition,
pervasive, expansive,
beyond any sort of labels or terminology,
this is what we, what we
have always been,
it is what we always will be;
It is not so simple to understand
when we are immersed in this body of distraction,
this cluster of oh-so-rasping-on-our-nerves nonsense,
this agitation that bludgeons us so hard
so hard that it takes our true breath
from us, our cognizance of this moment,
taking away our focus on the ultimate
away, taking our wisdom
simply
away;
The impossibility is thus that we ourselves
remove our own primordial knowledge
though it cannot be destroyed,
it is simply a figment of our vivid imagination
which arises as we convince ourselves
we convince ourselves that this world is real;
What is that?
That confusion that arises,
is it, is it
an aberration
in the brilliant
timeless
luminosity?
Oh no,
it can't be,
it must be
it must not be that!
It must be
rare
magical displays
the essence of all possibilities;
It must happen,
it must
it

must
because
all
is
good.

78

Those who have awakened to the presence
that presence of primordial luminosity
have opened themselves completely
opened their hearts and mind
fully, nakedly
to that spaciousness
of beyond, beyond now,
of beyond what we think of as
beyond,
beyond what we
rationally think
is possible,
going beyond
in such a way
that this small, feeble
silly being
that we think of as self
expands to infinite proportions;
Those awakened ones no longer think of self and other
as being constrained by each other or
existing in that way, separate, limited;
They see the all-good expanse
they see that amazing bright luminosity,
they see that as having no limitations,
not limited by self or other, or ideas,
not constrained by dogma or rules or conjecture,
seeing the real nature of things,
not being confused by ego
or notions of permanence
or notions of that that
that ridiculous idea of nothing
or thinking that this egotistical self is real
or thinking that this dream is real
or thinking that concepts have validity of any sort

when being omnipresently aware in that;
The reality of this world arising happens,
it happens only because of your mind
your mind telling itself that this is so
and that is so, convincing itself
that the illusory dream is real,
believing that that illusion must be so;
Without the confusion of mind
the world of suffering, Samsara,
could not arise
in the least, not in the least!
Remaining present in that knowledge
opens us to this very simple
awakening.

79

That amazing bright light
those expansive brilliant
teachings of wisdom beyond thought
supreme among all wisdom surrounding
wisdom surrounding, encompassing
our every waking moment;
That Dharma, supreme lessons
of magnificent light
extreme ultimate
core brightness blazing
in our heart of hearts, igniting,
cutting through infinitely in this moment
this expansive moment of great compassion,
our awakened mind resonates
in that booming moment
of recognition,
sending shockwaves
throughout;
All of
that,
that moment
when we awaken,
is happening now;
This is our time,
this is
when, when
that supreme knowledge

becomes
known
to
us.

80

Awareness cannot happen
without peace, we must rest in this moment,
we must become masters of calm abiding presence;
All our fixations, mind dancing
here and there, not resting,
becoming agitated over nothing whatsoever,
in this moment, all that nonsense
disturbs us, keeps us
in the continuity of moments, it keeps us
keeps us distracted
keeps us rattled
keeps us unsettled,
and anxious,
obsessed;
Peace
must happen first,
then insight into the moment,
then they must combine, by
continually going back to peace,
then opening the heart more and more,
then, at that time, glimpse that eternal
immutable timeless luminosity,
it is just there,
just there
so plainly obvious, all-pervasive, subtle;
Oh, wandering being,
being who has been so confused
for all eternity, from beginningless beginnings;
Look at how simple it really is,
such a subtle thing,
to awaken;
Why has that been such a mystery?
HO HO HO!!!
Better to laugh at this travesty,
it cannot be helped;
This condition, unchanging,

of pure awareness
has always been
just there
in
this
eternal
moment.

81

Folding
into this moment,
perfect liberation,
unending, spontaneous, naturally perfect,
the glow within the glow within ever-present luminosity
luminosity beyond all intensity of brightness
now
in this moment
this moment of self liberation
self-liberates
in that
that
amazing
magical array
of this eternal now;
All that we think
is real
liberates, karma liberates,
though we have been
woefully unaware
from timeless beginnings
paying no attention
whatsoever, heeding not
our real condition,
our real nature;
From beginningless time
all that, our state of being
has been ignored,
we have been
oblivious
to
that.

82

All of our actions occur
within this perfect timeless expansive field,
within our present environment, wherever that may be,
obscurations to knowing how that is,
knowing that pristine condition
are within this most perfect
state of being,
we cannot go
anywhere
where it is not perfect, perfection
from beyond beginnings, the beginning
from before beginnings
from beginningless time, beyond time
beyond origins of thought or ideas about time
or any of that assembled fabrication within
this perfect moment;
We have nowhere to go,
nothing to do,
and, yet,
we feel this need,
we yearn, we seek
we obsessively seek something, anything something
something perfectly meaningful along this path,
we seek to overcome
all that clouds our vision;
We are confused, anxious, agitated,
not knowing the meaning of this life,
not seeing just what is going on here,
not aware of our awareness;
Just look!
That timeless luminosity is present
at all times, being all good;
Just see!
See that perfect state
beyond all obscurations!
Be very still!
Still your mind!
It is not so hard to see,
just be still and look at that,
feel that, know that
that amazing

Dharmakaya;
Know
that our actions
cannot bring us closer
or send us further
away
from that timeless presence, that
ultimate bright
condition.

83

Preparing for death
we prepare to meet our real nature
perfect
existing as it is
beyond time
beyond timeless eternity
from beginningless beginnings
as it always has been
in death after death
after life after life
we prepare
for that
timeless
luminosity
beyond changing
not coming
or going
beyond
beyond
that primordial wisdom
that condition
that is so very familiar to us
that amazing brilliant luminosity beyond reason
that condition where we have always been, but
we keep forgetting that it is always so;

HO HO HO!!!

This existence can only make one laugh!
This state beyond reason
is always

here
just
as
it
is.

84

Though we may think we are
here or there
nothing
is as it seems;
Location
cannot be located,
self
cannot be found,
we see nothing to stand upon
in this constantly changing condition;
In this swirling ever-changing physical reality
this unreality of illusion,
that fictitious reality we create
for our self
a self we cannot locate, alone,
alone
alone where there is
no stability
whatsoever,
as every part of us changes
constantly vibrating buzzing twirling within this material form,
thoughts, like waves on the high seas,
dissolving, spinning, electrocuting this instant,
where we seek answers
seek answers
seek any answer to our most
precious concerns,
this life is
is not as it seems,
and we most definitely are not this
or that, here or there;
It is folly to seek pseudo-answers
blind nonsensical beliefs without examination
within this illusion, to
explain

what is not real,
within unreality trying to explain reality,
comically trying, ever-changing folly,
better, I think,
to see that
immutable
presence
of being, just
as it
is,
beyond
beyond all explanations
beyond any and all assertions,
of any kind.

85

This life
appearing out of timeless luminosity
may seem like pure shit
everything in it
may seem
as if
it is nothing other than
shit;
Reject this life
and it simply
comes back
with a worse stench;
How is it that you reject
negative appearances
that are none other than
arising out of your own mind?
Can you not see that you have
fabricated, created, subjugated
this appearance to be that way?
An idiot makes a claim,
and you believe it;
Life arises
as an illusion
out of the all-good,
the nature of mind, it
arises out of perfection,

not out of this delusion
you have created about
good and evil—that is nonsense!
Throw that stupid idea away!
It will bring you no benefit whatsoever,
it never has, with anyone
in this all-good
way of being;
Only you
place the
label.

86

Why do you cling
to those things
those ridiculous things you think
are pleasant?
Can you not see
that that
appears
only from mind's subjectivity?
Why do you push away,
rejecting what pains
your senses?
Are you insane?
Do you really have no idea that
that is unreal?
Let that go into that timeless
expansive space, luminous
beyond any brightness,
so brilliant, so intense
that that cannot be described
in any way;
Let all this swirling madness
go back to that
that infinite
primordial
state,
our
real
condition.

87

Timeless
immutable
not dependent upon space
beyond all constraints of time
beyond thoughts of expansiveness
containing all that we know, all
as only a small microscopic iota
barely there in that intense
luminous state beyond
beyond
beyond all that can be imagined
beyond all that is all,
this is our real
condition;
That infinite expanse is
just the first step
on our journey
home,
this place
where we
are
now.

88

Imagine
a field of pure white,
it's not snow or sunshine
it's not a land filled with diamonds,
it's not fire, though it is much brighter
than that;
Imagine that brightness
that all-consuming
radiant luminosity,
immense,
unbounded, eternal
expanding in all directions
forever,
and that bright expanse

has no ground,
no sky,
no horizon,
no up, no down,
time does not progress,
nor does it
digress;
It just is as it is,
more real than reality,
more intense than any
flash of lightning, or the core of any star,
or even a trillion stars,
brighter than that
much brighter
limitless,
open,
vividly occurring
when we
truly
rest.

89

Like a golden pearl
glistening in empty space,
not being held up, not falling,
neither coming nor going
not here nor there, not
lasting in the least,
not beyond, yet beyond
imagination,
not an object that
can be grasped, not an idea,
not nothing, not something,
but it is precious, all pervasive;
It is the openness of this
moment, awareness projecting itself
where nothing exists,
miraculous
appearances;

AH

Now, unlimited possibilities
vast infinite potentiality is seen here,
not where, not when,
there is nothing to do,
nothing
to dissolve,
nothing to create;
That most perfect state,
that eternal moment,
pervasive, omnipresent,
that timeless luminosity, is
seen clearly as
all
good
in this eternal
moment.

90

This arc of light
cutting through,
melding past, present and future,
burning bright outside of time
within time, beyond bright timeless consciousness,
now in this all-inclusive awareness
beyond dimensionality itself,
remains unchanged, clear,
cannot be liberated,
cannot be changed;
This is our perfect
primordial condition,
our real nature;
It is not self, or anyone in particular,
it is not ego speaking to us,
it is not some being
that we have discovered
on a distant world;
It is this
real, not real in the ordinary sense,
condition of the all-good,
it is what we encounter
when we die, or when we dream brightly,

clearly, when we are deep
in contemplation,
when we
let mind
become still,
or glimpse a clear moment,
being present in that
so that we can become
aware
of that,
of that unchanging
ultimate state of being,
that quality
of our real nature,
this state of being simply
as
it is.

91

More important than ideas
about emptiness
is that incredible spaciousness that is cognized
beyond openness, beyond space, beyond time,
in the motion of now unchanging,
being present in that;
Seen as bright magical appearance,
a grand brilliant reflection within the source,
the nature of this grand illusion
presents itself uncorrupted
uncorrupted by attachment
or ideas, or self;
Here in this stable condition
I see,
I see that
that motion of thought, energy,
I see that there is nothing stable
where consciousness forms,
or where attachment fixates to ideas
about this or that, or something that becomes
that, as waves reverberate in great swirls, crashing
energetic vibrations, beams of light
rays reflecting, cognizance vibrating

energetic colors shifting amid a field
a field of every possibility,
from this to that, sounds
booming, resonating,
all this commotion amid
that
that great unchanging
timeless luminosity
that extreme intense bright
beyond brightness
beyond space or time
beyond beyond
that, that, that
indescribableness.

92

Becoming that bright light, that fully aware luminosity,
inseparable from that amazing brightness
existent from timeless beginningless beginnings,
becoming that which is already present here
now, now beyond space and time,
primordial awareness, becoming not anything nor nothing
becoming what cannot be, becoming what cannot not be,
becoming that presence of ultimate truth
not becoming at all or not not becoming;
Any assertion at all has no place,
cannot stand on its own,
becomes meaningless,
it is utter nonsense pointing
at utter nonsense, insinuating
some crazy deluded idea,
pointing at itself without having anything
to point at, pointing pointing
just possessing
no conceivable way
to describe what that actually is
having no possible method
to explain
to fathom
to assert
because it is beyond
our usual way of thinking,

it is beyond
object
reason
thought
concept
or
delusion.

93

Tranquility bursts into that, that infinite open space, that timeless luminosity,
BOOM!
Suddenly fully aware we find lasting peace
within that expansive now where we become integrated with intense light,
within that dimension that is neither inner nor outer,
not out there, not this, nor that,
vast, incomparable, beyond any sort of
spatial constraint or limitation, beyond
beyond reason;
Finding tranquility, we rest,
seeing now as it is, gazing in the ultimate rested state we
discover openness;
We see now, blossoming into
that, with a solid BOOM, the earth shakes,
recognition of mind seeing its true nature,
within this immense dimension,
where there is no limit
to that, unlimited potentiality;
Moment passing to moment,
great tranquility
permeates the very fabric of this aware condition,
and the next moment we see, as we completely relax,
we see that same illuminated peace,
opening us to the nature of all
that can be, the essence of all;
Tranquility passing
between moments,
within a peaceful now, we see that
see that it is that indescribable that,
appearing as empty reality,
just that, nothing more,
nothing less,
not everything,

not not everything,
inseparable,
not two,
not really even one, just
one taste, an essence,
ultimate appearance;
Now becomes
what is
next, and before,
halcyon of light
love compassion,
tranquil
now.

94

We see apparitions, thinking they will last,
poking them, as if they are solid,
smelling, tasting, listening, thinking about them
and, then, there is this nature of those things
the essence, which is beyond our senses, beyond thoughts which define that;
So we see that place where delusion comes in contact
with this ineffable reflection of that delusion;
Mind
and the nature of mind,
not two, inseparable, radiant, miraculous;
This clarity of being aware of that is radiant
in the extreme explosive brilliance
of that moment
when mind and nature of mind
are realized as one,
mind merging with nature of mind,
the reflection and the source,
one essence, one view,
one, just one
one, inseparable always,
just that amazing openness
when this physical world seems to dissolve,
when bright rays of light, vibration, swirling madness
opens to that bright timeless expanse;
Then we realize we have
been here all along,
in this condition,

this reality is not
other than
here
now,
it is simply
as
it
is.

95

HO HO HO!!!
This that, this life, this condition,
is self-perfected now!
Such a tremendous joke to witness!!!
This essence of all meaning,
these appearances that have caused us so much worry,
they are nothing other than what has been
will be, never has been, timeless
from beginningless time!!!
Such an utter contradiction
dashing all of our concepts to dust,
this self-person, personhood
is just an imaginary appearance
within an imaginary appearance
within an illusion
within a dream
and another dream
and another life filled with dreams;
HA!
What joke could bring
all this together
in a bigger way than that?!
HA HA HA HA HO!!
Clap your hands,
spin around in the dance of your lifetime,
enter that burst of energy with laughter,
all is liberated
here now
in this
very
funny
moment.

96

Immutable
indestructible
that condition, that indescribable condition,
that condition of our cognizant awareness
within mind, beyond mind, reflecting
that radiant empty essence of all things and beyond
cognizant beyond any sort of reification
beyond any thought or label
beyond any impermanence
beyond, beyond permanence,
beyond those ideas that bind us to this illusion,
this cosmic joke, this magical condition, this dream,
how can any of that become anything
that could be dissolved or removed
or crushed or exploded or expanded out of existence,
or how could it be harmed in any way?
How could that
become something that could ever be
destroyed?
Here in the bardo of death
we see our real condition,
expanse of luminous mind beyond reason;
We are completely open
to that, to
to that perfect state of being
luminous, open to that condition
that has always been present
from before beginningless beginnings,
we see the origin of our essence,
of our real nature, of our
brilliance;
Here we see, we know,
the nature of all, the essence of that,
timelessly beyond
all imperfect
knowledge,
delusion
or useless beliefs;
We see that
as
it
is.

97

Beyond birth, old age and death,
our real condition
remains timelessly
luminous,
as is,
it remains
constant beyond ideas,
our real condition remains
perpetually bright
completely open, extremely luminous,
brilliant, beyond time
or space;
This natural condition
is not to be
moved
not budged in the least,
it cannot be changed, it is indestructible;
It is not possible for that to become
something, anything, nothing,
it is not an object,
it is not a thing to be recognized;
It is beyond such things of mind, such points of confusion,
such limited human ideas about this or that,
it is beyond being something we can explain,
it is really beyond something that we
can point towards, it is not like that;
It just is as it is in this timeless luminous
condition of spacelessness
that remains completely
unchanged;
Things change,
our real condition
does not;
It is
as
it
is.

98

From all of this evil and confusion, this world of strife,
this mire and mud of delusion,
from all that hatred and destruction, and desire,
cruelty inherent in this world of powerful men
and angry women, from all of that,
all the ignorant beasts of every sort, the gods, and hell beings,
and all those who are too numerous to mention,
from this world of ego, where tears manifest,
manifesting from all of this pain and death,
from all of this torture, this contrivance,
that cannot be ended by death nor seeing others die,
nor by killing oneself, nor through old age,
nor by controlling others, nor through revolution,
there is no escape, it just keeps happening around us, in us, in our mind,
actions appearing in a flurry of agitation, no matter what we do,
except by going to the root cause of this condition, ignorance, ego,
karma, mind, there is nothing else that we can do about this amazing
magical display that has caused us so much misery throughout untold eons;
When we die, when the inevitable happens to us,
the next life brings exactly the same problems, we drift
forever and ever, forever through this cycle of existence;
Without addressing the root of the problem, we will only have
more of the same, the next life brings all that had been vexing us as
before, with the added problems of why we did that disturbance,
that unspeakable act of violence or that word of anger
making things much worse for our own precious life
and the lifetimes to follow in an endless array;
There is no escape, unless we look
unless we look inwardly at mind,
recognizing the nature of mind,
liberating that which binds us;
We cannot find any escape, whatsoever,
so, rise
from this cesspool, this stench,
arise
from this stink, this toil and swill,
this torment;
Enter that pristine state
for all-time, for all-good,
for all eternity remain in that beyond, just remain as it is, in that
that pure essence of light, of awareness that is all-good

remaining in this condition that is our true nature,
that has always been just there, indescribable,
surrounding all, within all,
though we had not noticed,
radiant beginningless compassion,
timelessly luminous, just as it is, as it was,
as it will be, beyond illusion when passing
from one life
to the
next.

99

Knowing that we are indestructible,
among these indescribable conditions of mind and the nature of mind,
knowing that,
knowing that we have developed this
enlightenment attitude,
knowing all that,
having found the nature of mind,
discovered this cosmic joke,
knowing that we are present in that;
It is time to become fearless,
time to develop inner strength,
undeniable courage standing against any and all
demons, any fear of destruction or obstruction,
any and all that stands in our way, make friends with that;
It is time to open our heart and mind
to the inevitable forces that will rush in;
We can confidently, abundantly without hesitation,
become ferocious, become that strength
that is beyond fear
or concern about personal safety;
Staring into the abyss of death
nothing can shake this new-found wisdom, of opening
to this attitude of indestructability,
of deathlessness,
of this great strength;
This undying heroism cannot be swayed
by worries about death,
the real condition of this illusion has been realized!
Staring fearlessly into the condition of our
certain demise, seeing death for what it is, remaining quite relaxed,

we conquer that condition
completely;
Seeing the bardos of life and death,
seeing that for what it is,
what is there to fear?
We see this at last, with clarity
as we gaze into timeless luminosity
seeing at last our real deathless condition,
we can no longer be conquered,
we can no longer
fear our everlasting
oppressor, we
take refuge
in our own
timeless wisdom;
Seen at last
we become
present
in
that.

100

Incomparable bliss, beyond
beyond all understanding of bliss,
energetic arising
from this physical presence,
within that ultimate state,
that ultimate state without any sort of constraint
without limitations of time or space,
beyond any conceptual understanding,
within this perfect moment,
this perfect perpetual instantaneous condition,
self-liberating, absolute, beyond
beyond such feeble notions created by humankind
we see life articulated in a cycle
of living and dreaming and dying,
and we see that that means nothing,
it is merely an illusion of our own creation;
This articulated wisdom and bliss
of our relative condition
does not compare
to that ultimate

state of bliss
of an open heart
an open mind
held by nothing,
never limited,
with total
freedom,
bliss
unending.

101

Here we are in this greatly limited delusion,
ignorantly thinking that this is real,
then looking towards death
and the nature of mind
we see how this energetic condition
of being is so much more than that,
and looking further into that condition of extreme luminosity
we see clearly
that our real condition is timeless
that our real state is luminous,
so bright that we cannot confine it to reason;
We cannot limit what we encounter to mere thoughts about this or that,
we see with absolute clarity
that the nature of our true condition
is beyond
beyond all such limitations, beyond all thought
beyond, beyond concepts or objects
or this or that greatly constrained philosophy;
We see vastness, open beyond the idea of vastness,
beyond letting go of these or those notions,
we see that it cannot be reified
or described in any way;
We cannot limit this view
to our finger pointing in this direction or that direction,
it is not limited by spatial constraints or vectors or locality,
it is not limited, nor can we it locate that by points in time;
It is not between objects or in objects or both or neither;
Any limitation is just more grasping,
not understanding,
having no real knowledge of unlimited potentiality,
not having that

knowledge,
that knowledge of what is beyond all
grasping,
grasping at some arbitrary knowledge of ideas,
limiting in any way
through
definitions,
definitions of that
which cannot be
cannot be
defined,
simply
beyond
all of
that.

102

Illumination
from within, from within
this corpse, this aging agitation
repugnance in motion festering as it ages, this body
this mind within this condition of physical mayhem impermanently disrupting
its actual condition
falling apart as it takes one step into the future,
flooded by thoughts of this and of that thing
that is not true,
illumination happens all around,
and why do we miss it?
All this brightness in each moment is lost
to things that do not matter;
We look here, we look there, not finding,
not remembering what we were looking for,
not forgetting any thought which we never really had,
thinking thoughts are important, even though they served us
rarely;
Here we are
confused,
alone,
stupid,
dull,
angry,
not understanding any of it,

not
seeing,
not being aware
of this moment;
We miss it, this magnificent illumination, if
if we cannot see this moment
this moment, this moment, clearly
clearly happening;
We miss it, we miss it
altogether,
even
though
it
is
all.

103

These sleeping Buddhas
are all the same, identical, every last one of them,
really just identical, having been perfect from the beginning,
they slumber, they sleep,
they nervously fixate through this cloudy dream on all this noisy nonsense;
What is this awakening, if it is anything?
Once a Buddha, always a Buddha,
and so they are, here they sleep
among us all in all their unsatisfactory restlessness, our restlessness;
What difference does it make if they awaken or not!?
They can keep sleeping, for all I care!
It will make no difference whatsoever,
it will make no difference,
not to anyone, not
to the nature of mind, the essence of all things,
which is indestructible
perfect
from the beginning, absolutely perfect,
unchangeable,
why should it matter?
Why, well of course it matters!
This slumber from beginningless beginnings
has never been satisfying for anyone, it creates great unnecessary
suffering,
this slumber

can be a nightmare, extremely painful from
time to time, or
it can be simply unsatisfying, this illusion,
for eons upon eons,
this dream, this illusion
of life from which escape seems impossible
is none other than a crazy cyclone of disturbing emotions
spinning us all around for all eternity,
not really life, not really death, not really a dream;
What is that?
A sleeping Buddha cannot awaken
without choosing,
one must choose to leave cyclic existence, all on our own;
Great compassion for self, then for others, the first step, the ultimate step,
it is all the key to it all, ultimate true compassion emanating from timeless
beginnings;
After that,
anything is possible,
anything
ANYTHING!
It is not
limited in any way,
potentiality, our utter potentiality
it is infinite for a Buddha
who has
awakened;
We are all as that.

104

Dharmakaya
present
in every moment
open expanse
of mind meeting
nature of mind,
as when we die,
as when we dream,
as when we are born,
that tremendous
illumination beyond
utterly open, complete

ever-present, always,
without being constrained
by ideas or time or space,
with unlimited potentiality
emptiness embodying truth,
ultimate truth, the mind of the Buddhas,
that which we always encounter clearly
each time we die, as we pass through
that bardo of realization presenting itself;
yet, if we do not recognize that, what we see,
we will remain unaware, remaining in this cycle,
from one lifetime, to the next lifetime, to the next
forever in that cycle, poisoned by our own doing,
not seeing that each moment is totally complete
complete, surrounded by that amazing wisdom,
that brilliance, all-pervasive, encompassing all,
all-good perfection that is timelessly luminous
bright beyond our wildest imagined thought
of what we think is utterly intense brightness
brightness beyond any brightness
we have ever seen within our
magical illusion of life;
Only the Buddhas
can see clearly
at all times
this display
of pristine
beauty,
this perfect
empty
essence
of
truth.

105

Sambhogakaya
enjoyment aspect embodied, realized
in this cognizant nature of being
fully enjoyed
energetically formed potential
amid light and colors dancing
rays and sounds emerging

in that state of consciousness that has emerged
from that perfect timeless illumination;
Aryas and Bodhisattvas delight
in complete bliss, in the presence of celestially appearing Buddhas,
while contemplating this dimension,
singing, dancing amid rays of light, tigles
full of unbounded joy;
Though we could not be without this
energetic consciousness,
without this swirling manifestation
of dynamic realization,
our physical form
could not possibly appear without that, it could not appear
from pure timeless luminosity,
each moment forming
such delight as this, relies upon
cognizant awareness,
and the aspect of this energetic condition
this nonmaterial energetic condition that brings us into
a celestial body, unbounded form, beyond space and time;
Without such delight manifesting in pure enjoyment
nothing can appear as we know it,
unlimited joy
such as that
remains in our very being,
even when unaware,
it is that manifestation
of the enjoyment body unhindered,
it is that condition of bliss,
nirvana of the mind,
which is inherently attached
to our world, not beyond
beyond, just hidden
barely hidden, except to those
passing through the death bardo, birth, dreams,
seen by those with trauma
or extreme pleasure,
or reclusive gurus remaining in equipoise,
or upon awakening,
seen
by
mind.

106

Nirmanakaya
What can we say this physical dimension?
This illusion, this illusory material world of angst
this world of great suffering
is perfect,
perfect from the beginning
from the beginning
perfection;
Here we are in this physical body,
thinking this physical world is real,
suffering, lamenting in many many ways
from beginningless time, stuck in this cycle, trapped in
time space, and it is not real;
This is the realm
of those beings
beings who are anxious, uneasy,
unable to see this magical illusion unfolding,
beings who are unable to see the obvious,
confused by aversion, by attachment,
ignorant to the real nature of all;
This is the realm of those confused beings
who cannot see clearly
they cannot really know whenever a Buddha appears; This
this realm keeps us from seeing what we really are;
This is the realm where we can hear a Buddha speak,
only if we open our hearts just a little;
This world, this ghastly violent messy world of turmoil, of nervous dreams
unending,
of anxious thoughts of fear, of anger, ignorance, pride and desire,
cyclic in nature, this world of confusion, of constant unease and attachment,
this is where it is possible to go beyond,
and yet beings resist that, so insane they are that they refuse
to go beyond, to escape, if only they knew how rare this chance really was,
if only we were open to that, if only we
opened our hearts and mind, opening
just kept opening, opening until until our heart fully opens, our
hearts our mind awaken, becoming
open to that to that, that
magnificent amazing
awakening, that realization
that has always

been perfectly
just
here,
just here
now.

107

HO HO HO!

Utter joy has arisen in the spectacle of it all,
may those serious wandering seekers, those fortunate ones
who have discovered the path to liberation,
those who are full of such heavy anxiety and dread,
see at once
the nature of life and dreams
and death, see the illusion of it all, see
through this great laughter, see
through radiant joy emerging from this grand spectacle,
from timeless luminosity, beyond thought,
wisdom that is expanse of mind and the nature of mind, see
see that these cannot be separated.

Why did we think it was not so?

Dreams unfolding cannot be separated by
or from this magical illusion of our daily lives.
There is no difference whatsoever!
Dreams and daily life and death, they are all the same.
What happens when we look for death?
It cannot be found, nor should it be believed.
Just let that illusion go!
Do not believe this dream, this illusion, this magical appearance,
this death or life, this flash of light in your mind!
Do not believe for an instant that that is real!
Open indescribable indestructible inconceivable
extremely intense brilliant luminosity beyond thought and time,
see that that is here now, see that!
See that that is surrounding your conscious essence, for you to realize, that,
that is now in this present moment for you to see with complete clarity,
it is your true nature of being, see that!
beyond this shaky body, beyond

beyond this aging useless corpse!

When the door opens don't hesitate,
integrate yourself completely with timeless luminosity;
Have no fear!
Move quickly when the door opens!

Time is nothing whatsoever!
Space is nothing whatsoever!
This life, nothing whatsoever!
Death is also nothing whatsoever;

Do not cling to samsara,
or any beliefs that uphold this world around you;
Do not cling to nirvana,
nor to the inner reflections of peace and utter bliss;
All of that traps us in a cycle
of birth and rebirth, of sickness and aging
and dreams;
It must be seen as delusion, for that is what it really is;
This life, and death, is nothing other than an illusion unfolding,
in this continuous moment of suffering unending,
forever.

If you seek liberation, then integrate all of this magical display
into the true manifestation that has been perfect from the beginning,
of that bright timeless luminosity, of the true nature of mind,
in this turbulence of now unending.
Do not cling to this life, or all that is precious to you, not even an iota;
Do not reject that which has harmed you, or that which terrifies to the core;
rather, rather just let all of that propel you, effortlessly, with joy,
remaining completely at ease, relaxed, remaining where you already are,
let it propel you without moving anywhere, without the slightest effort,
into the true nature of mind, open, free, without limitations,
without bias of any kind.
Do not cling to any who have been there for you, nor those who call you
dear,
nor those who have done you wrong, nor those who have forced you to
believe this or that;
rather, walk away into self-liberation,
with utter unshakable courage.
Do not cling to this world in the least,
go beyond, let this abide in all its beauty, and ugliness, and terror;
See that these appearances are none other than self-fabrication, ego
manifestations,

actively engaged ignorance, samsara, mind's own
construct.
When you are ready, and have done all of that,
when confidence manifests
in your being, and you see the nature of mind,
when you recognize that, all that amazing essence, a glimpse of
Dharmakaya,
rest completely, naturally, in this dream-like apparition,
go beyond, while at ease, while remaining,
go beyond the indescribable, despite the turbulent chaos,
go beyond beyond.
Conquer death, all aspects of death,
awaken completely,
go beyond beyond beyond,
beyond being, or belief, being
present in that instantaneously appearing moment,
timelessly luminous
forever.

108

What is that bright sky?

AH

It is not out there,
it is in here,
yet, it is not in here either, nor is it both,
it is not this or that,
not other, not neither, not the same,
it is beyond what is, both and neither, beyond
what can be added or negated,
it cannot be located
in either time or space, where can it be?
That bright spacious sky,
brilliant beyond a thousand stars,
brighter than all universes
together in one dot, utter openness expanding
expanding forever into now, that brightness
that, that amazing thatness
that cannot be explained, not not explained,
not different, not separate,

glowing from within, utter intensity beyond reason,
I can see that I have never gone away, from that;
In this present explosive radiant nowness,
as I dedicate this perfect merit
to all beings,
to protectors,
to guardians,
to dakas as well as all dakinis,
to wisdom beings and the guru
of this timelessly luminous path,
my perfect guru who is really just primordial
nature of mind,
I can see
that I have seen
all of that before,
in death and life and dreams, always
forever
in this amazing
ever-present
instantaneously always
clearly eternal
all-good
perfect
now.

AFTERWARDS

The practice of *Tögal* is often referred to in Dzogchen practice, as being essential to awakening. It is the practice of directly accessing the ultimate light of Dharmakaya, of crossing over into having that direct experience, as well as having that ultimate knowledge of all three of the kayas, of having spontaneous presence in life. Without a teacher pointing out our real nature and transmitting that knowledge, helping us to implement practices for awakening, it is extremely unlikely that a person could remain in this knowledge. It would also be nearly impossible to awaken without on-going practice. It is essential that we practice in such a way that we prepare ourselves for the ultimate, making ourselves ready for death. Having found a glimpse of the ultimate, then we need to practice in such a way that reminds us of what we have discovered, bringing us back to our real condition, over and over again, until it becomes natural and continuous.

The whole experience of having a Near Death Experience provides us with access to the light of Dharmakaya. When we return to our lives, this quickly fades into distant memories, which become forgotten, overtaken by our somewhat unsettling lives. Our lives, however unfortunately, soon become cluttered and overwhelmed by fixations and distractions, our grasping at what is not real, filled with disturbing emotions and embroiled with conflict. We quickly forget the unlimited qualities of our real nature, upon entering our life once more, upon engaging in life in the usual way. We soon forget that nondual presence, which seemed so very real to us. We go back to our old habits of deluding ourselves.

Tögal is really going from ordinary life into our natural luminous state. My experience, as described within this book, goes from that natural state of Dharmakaya light back into this cluttered ordinary life. It is really Tögal in reverse. That was my experience, that which I realized upon returning from timeless luminosity, Dharmakaya awareness.

That is the experience that rang very strongly with me, that which I was reminded of when I practiced or sang the Song of the Vajra, or even when I remained present throughout my day and night. I came out of death with great confidence and an awareness of our real condition in each moment, no matter what I was doing. Even in dreams, this awareness did not diminish.

In reality, when we become integrated into the light, we awaken. This happens to us all. It is more than typical; rather, it is guaranteed to happen. We all have a taste of remaining as an enlightened being each time we die, even if it is just a brief flash of light. This is very ordinary, not unusual in the least. It happens to us all—repeatedly throughout cyclic existence.

If we have not prepared for living our lives as enlightened beings, then we quickly forget the gift of having died and then returned to life. The realization of our true condition, timeless luminosity, fades quickly, if we do not know how to remain in that condition in life. It is that our distractions in life quickly take over with relative ease, leading to more of the same sort of suffering, confusion and anxiety that we have been experiencing for uncounted lifetimes, through an unending array of eons, from beginningless time and this continuous cycle which traps us.

I laughed and laughed, when I realized that this is the case. We take everything so seriously; and, yet, here is this cosmic joke, playing itself out, over and over again. How could we have missed something so obvious?

Here we are trapped in cyclic existence, and there is really absolutely no reason that we should be trapped. We create our own cage. We fabricate our own demise. We build our constraints with imaginary limitations that are not real. We lament that we cannot return, even though we have never left. The whole world is insane like this. All we can do is laugh, there is nothing else to do when we get what is really happening here in this imaginary existence.

Samsara, or our confused state which is poisoned by ignorance, attraction and aversion, that we think of as this world, filled with disturbing emotions and attachment to what is not real, is not a tragedy, it is more like a beautiful comedy. None of this is real, we only think it is real. Like a dream, it quickly disperses into emptiness, the present moment is gone before it arrives. It was never really there; and, yet, we have lamented our lives every day. We worried about how we could stay safe, even though we are truly indestructible. We saw the ugliness of this world, thinking that it held the answers, and we became truly disappointed that answers could not be found. We failed to live with love and compassion, then became upset by this, instead of just going to the root of what caused this, our own deluded mind that has become poisoned.

Intuitively, we all know that love and compassion emanate from the light of wisdom. We know this without having to be told. It is why we regret our actions in life, or why we cover up our actions from ourselves, not wanting to face what we are actually doing. Rather than developing great compassion in our lives, we continue as before, and this is exactly what prevents us from becoming aware of our real condition. Bodhicitta is the key to everything.

In the ultimate sense, our real condition is pure radiant compassion beyond measure. We cannot stay immersed in this turbulent relationship we have with karma, expecting to awaken in that way. If we wish to awaken, we must begin with compassion for ourselves, then compassion for others, then letting it all go into a state of Ultimate Bodhicitta, Timeless Luminosity.

SONG of the VAJRA

E MA KI RI KĪ RĪ
MA-SU TA VA LI VĀ LĪ
SA-MI TA SU RU SŪ RŪ
KU-TA LI MA SU MĀ SŪ
E KA RA SU LI BHA ṬA YE
CI KI RA BHU LI BHA ṬHA YE
SA MUN TA CA-RYA SU GHA YE
BHE TA SA NA BHYA KU LA YE
SA KA RI DHU KA NA
MA TA RI VAI TA NA
PA RA LI HI SA NA
MA KAR TA KHE LA NAM
SAM BHA RA THA ME KHA CAN TA PA
SŪR YA BHA TA RAI PA SHA NA PA
RA NA BI DHI SA GHU RA LA PA
MAS MIN SA GHU LĪ ṬA YA PA
GHU RA GHŪ RĀ SA GHA KHAR ṆA LAM
NA RA NĀ RĀ I THA PA ṬA LAM
SIR ṆA SĪR ṆĀ BHE SA RAS PA LAM
BHUN DHA BHŪN DHĀ CHI SHA SA KE LAM
SA SĀ
RI RĪ
LI LĪ
I Ī
MI MĪ
RA RA RĀ

*As transmitted to me by my root guru, Chögyal Namkhai Norbu Rinpoche, the *Song of the Vajra* is both a song and a mantra, practiced by many Dzogchen practitioners around the world, found in the *Tantra of the Coalescence of Sun and Moon*, and *The Tibetan Book of the Dead*. This transmission, which is written in the language of Oddiyana, was also transmitted to Namkhai Norbu by his teacher, in this way, in a line going back to the time of Vairocana, perhaps further. The teachings of it are considered to be secret; however, my teacher decided it should be taught in the West, before it is lost altogether. To receive full benefit, transmission is needed.

ACKNOWLEDGEMENTS

I would really like to thank my wife Lori, who supported my efforts for completing this work, as well as being right there during my heart procedure. It would have been impossible for me to complete the task of describing what had happened, as well as completing all of the poetry, if she had not accepted the idea that I needed to focus on this project, rather than my architecture career, for an extensive period of time. This created some economic uncertainty for us, which she endured without complaint, giving me much space and encouragement to complete this endeavor.

I would also like to thank my family for showing so much support, ever since I had my Near Death Experience. Much of this involved going through difficult times, while my health improved. Family stepped in when I needed them to be there, and I was in frequent contact with so many people from throughout my extended family.

I should also thank Keith Dowman, who helped me in so many ways, gave me advice after my NDE and encouraged me, when I needed encouragement. Receiving his feedback as this work came into focus was very important to me. Without Keith's additional encouragement to publish this work, I am not certain I would have been able to take the last few steps necessary. The work had become daunting, taking all of my energy to complete.

Of course, the other people I should also thank are those medical staff who kept my body from dying. Their professionalism and attentiveness brought me back, so then I was then able to describe what had happened.

As with all creative endeavors, many people, too numerous to mention, really helped to create the conditions of moral support and prompting that are needed. The work is not truly my own effort, it was because of a community of people who knew me and offered encouragement. My friends Gail Gaebe, MD, as well as Hugh and Cheryl Reitan, encouraged me along the way, as did many people from throughout the Dzogchen and Buddhist communities, as well as several people who have had NDE's, as well as those who wanted to learn more about such experience.

Thank you everyone, so very much, from the bottom of my heart. I cannot possibly know everyone who made this all possible. You all have my eternal gratitude.

REFERENCED, RELATED and RECOMMENDED:

Coleman, Graham, translated by Gyurme Dorje, *Meditations on Living, Dying and Loss: The Essential Tibetan Book of the Dead,* New York, Viking Penguin, 2008.

Coleman, Graham and Thupten Jinpa, translated by Gyurme Dorje, *The Tibetan Book of the Dead: First Complete Translation,* New York, Penguin Books, 2005. (Originally composed by Padmasambhava.)

Dorje, Choying Tobden, translated by Gyurme Dorje, *The Complete Nyingma Tradition from Sutra to Tantra, Books 15 to 17*, Boulder, Snow Lion, 2016.

Dowman, Keith, *Old Man Basking in the Sun*, Kathmandu, Vajra Publications, 2007.

Mingyur, Yongey Rinpoche, *The Joy of Living*, New York, Harmony Books, 2007.

Khenpo, Nyoshul and Surya Das, *Natural Great Perfection: Dzogchen Teachings & Vajra Songs*, Ithaca, Snow Lion, 2008.

Norbu, Chogyal Namkhai and John Shane, *The Crystal and the Way of Light: Sutra, Tantra and Dzogchen*, Boston, Snow Lion, 2000.

Norbu, Chogyal Namkhai and John Shane, edited by Adriano Clemente, *Dzogchen: The Self-perfected State*, Ithaca, Snow Lion, 1996.

Norbu, Chogyal Namkhai and Fabio Maria Risolo, *Guruyoga*, Arcidosso, Shang Shung, 2011. (Restricted: transmission required.)

Norbu, Chogyal Namkhai and Adriano Clemente, *The Supreme Source: The Kunjed Gyalpo: The Fundamental Tantra of Dzogchen Semde*, Ithaca, Snow Lion, 1999.

Orofino, Giacomella, *Sacred Teachings on Death and Liberation: Texts from the most ancient traditions of Tibet*, Bridport, Prism Press, 1990.

Thurman, Robert F, *The Tibetan Book of the Dead*, New York, Bantam Books, 1994. (Originally composed by Padmasambhava.)

Urgyen, Tulku Rinpoche, translated & compiled by Erik Pema Kunsang & Marcia Binder Schmidt, *Quintessential Dzogchen: Confusion Dawns as Wisdom,* Hong Kong, Rangjung Yeshe Publications, 2006.

ABOUT the AUTHOR

Robert Aho currently lives in a secluded pine forest, on a lake in Northern Minnesota, with wolves, deer and other wildlife always close by. Although he has had several Buddhist teachers, of various backgrounds, his main practice is Dzogchen, which is sometimes called the ninth Yana, or vehicle, of Buddhist practice. Robert has led meditation groups, providing meditation instruction sometimes two or three times a week, written weekly newsletters on meditation teachings and organized many meditation retreats. As part of his daily life, Robert practices architecture, and has done numerous activities related to this, been a leader in professional organizations, given talks, written articles and newsletters, organized and led events. Robert also keeps busy with a wide variety of various creative endeavors, such as poetry, prose, painting and photography.

OM DHARE DHARE BHANDHARE SVĀHĀ
JAYA JAYA SIDDHI SIDDHI PHALA PHALA
HĂ A HA SHA SA MA MAMAKOLIṄ SAMANTA

Made in the USA
Middletown, DE
13 December 2021

55638111R00099